THE 10-SECOND JAILBREAK

The

The Helicopter Escape
of Joel David Kaplan

10-Second
Jailbreak

ELIOT ASINOF, WARREN HINCKLE,
AND WILLIAM TURNER

Holt, Rinehart and Winston

NEW YORK   CHICAGO   SAN FRANCISCO

Published simultaneously in Canada by Holt, Rinehart and Winston of Canada, Limited.

ISBN: 0-03-001011-x

Library of Congress Catalog Card Number: 72-78111

First Edition

Printed in the United States of America

Designed by Ronald Farber
Portions of this book appeared in different form in *Playboy* magazine.

Contents

8 pages of photographs follow page 116

Preface

During the last decade, in all the prisons of Mexico there was no man richer or more in pursuit of his freedom than an American named Joel David Kaplan—a strange, shy molasses heir who was serving a twenty-eight year sentence for the unsubstantiated murder of his partner in the gunrunning business, Luis Vidal, Jr.

Kaplan's status changed dramatically from that of millionaire loser to instant folk hero when, on August 18, 1971, he escaped from Santa Marta Acatitla Prison in authentic James Bond fashion: he was flown out in a supercharged helicopter, taking his cellmate along for the ride.

Kaplan then went underground in the United States. He was seen in the year following his escape only by his rescuers, his lawyers, and the authors.

During the nine-and-a-half years of his Kafkaesque struggle to get out of prison, few people in the United States knew of Kaplan's predicament; of those, fewer still cared. The Kaplan watchers were an odd lot by any standards: members of his feuding, sugar-rich family, some of whom wanted him out, while others preferred him where he was; agents of the American CIA and the Cuban G-2; and several frustrated journalists, a descriptive phrase to which the authors answer.

The first attempts to translate the *non sequitur*s of Kaplan's strange imprisonment into some sort of conspiratorial sense began more than five years ago in the offices of *Ramparts*. A crusading if financially shaky magazine under the editorship of Warren Hinckle, *Ramparts* had revived the ancient art of muckraking. If the early muckrakers had aimed at big business, *Ramparts*' target was big government, and, within the government, the CIA was of special interest, offering a journalistic game plan that won many celebrated scoops. It also brought on what some called an overdose of paranoia. Of no case was this more true than the Joel Kaplan affair, which was weird from the outset.

It began when William Turner, a Senior Editor on the magazine and a former FBI special agent, got word from a Brooklyn waiter that he had evidence Luis Vidal, Jr., had had important ties to the CIA. In the end, the waiter heatedly accused Turner of being a CIA agent out to sap his "vital juices." But some of the leads he had suggested did check out; in fact, many dovetailed with an independent investigation *Ramparts* was then mounting into the complicated affairs of Joel Kaplan's uncle, financier J. M. Kaplan, whose charitable foundation had already been exposed as a CIA conduit for the clandestine transmission of funds to domestic organizations and Caribbean politicians. It was an investigation that began when a former employee of J. M. Kaplan secretly approached Hinckle and Turner. In the course of furtive meetings in New York City, the ex-employee presented a picture of J. M. Kaplan—backed up with pounds of documents Xeroxed from the old man's files —that suggested, among other things, that there might be a connection between the multimillionaire uncle and his convicted-murderer nephew, with the CIA somewhere in the middle.

In July, 1967, Turner went to Mexico City. Posing as a Kaplan relative, Turner visited Joel in the medieval-appearing prison of Lecumberri. In his diary, he wrote:

I knew enough to take only the money I needed for taxi fare since wallets and other personal items had to be surrendered to the guards, some of whom were notoriously light-fingered. Inside the prison . . . a mariachi band strolled aimlessly while prisoners proudly displayed arts and crafts they had produced for outside sale. . . .

Joel was brought in . . . we had fifteen minutes, with a guard sitting a few feet away in apparent disinterest. Joel was pale and gaunt, with a saffron tinge that might have resulted from the siege of hepatitis. His handshake was limp and clammy, and he seemed to possess the edginess of a man waiting for the other shoe to fall.

His remarks were cryptic, to say the least. He just looked blank when I asked him if he were a CIA agent. He claimed his partner wasn't really dead. He kept mentioning Havana, saying I'd get some answers there. He said he'd been framed, but seemed reluctant to say who had framed him. "Somebody else's money was involved," he kept repeating. I asked whose money. The guard shrugged a halt to the interview, and Joel was led away.

The next two years were spent trying to throw light on the case, and especially on the CIA connection. The more questions asked, the less anyone even remotely involved wanted to talk. Those who did talk sought refuge in that gray area of speech between little white lies and big black ones. Joel Kaplan himself obviously knew a great deal more than he was willing to say. The truth was somewhere in the middle of a very big and very dirty puddle filled with the overflow of intelligence operations, general Caribbean intrigue, and greed and graft centering on gunrunning, dope smuggling, prostitution rings, and all the other businesses listed on the central exchange of the international black market. It was all very interesting and certainly puzzling, but insufficient for even Walter Winchell to go to press with.

Yet another year passed. *Ramparts* went into a financial decline and became a smaller magazine. Hinckle launched a new muckraking magazine, *Scanlan's*, which then picked up the case. Turner, taxing his patience, took up the tortuous assignment of retracing the paths he'd followed before. He was led only into some new box canyons. The best that *Scanlan's* could do was come up with several mutually exclusive theories on the Kaplan case—the few known facts supporting them all.

It appeared that the only way to get to the bottom of the Kaplan business was to break Joel out of prison and get him to talk as a free man. To that end, Hinckle approached Joel's sister, Judy Dowis, in the fall of 1970. Meetings were held. Hinckle even involved Hal Lipset, the legendary San Francisco private eye. Escape plans were hatched . . . and buried. And *Scanlan's* joined the infant mortality statistics of 1971.

Additional months passed. And then it happened. The escape of the century.

While scores of other reporters thundered by fruitlessly in a wild journalistic posse in search of Kaplan, William Turner and Warren Hinckle picked up the phone. Shortly afterward, they were meeting with Joel in his stateside hiding place. Not really so astonishing: five years on a story should give a reporter a few leads.

This book, however, is not the Gospel according to Joel Kaplan. After so many years of following false leads in pursuit of a story so strange that at times half-truths seemed the only constructive grammar, it was decided that the authors could rely on no single source in telling this story but would relate only those facts that could be objectively verified. It was also decided that the Kaplan saga needed a fresh eye, and at this point, Eliot Asinof joined the team. It would take the three authors a year of additional work to complete their investigations.

This book is, then, the product of that peculiar

phenomenon of modern letters known as "team journalism." It turned out to be a task which taxed the resources of the form. The milieu of illegal activities and intelligence operations in which this story unfolds made it doubly difficult, even for three writers, to separate the wheat of fact from the chaff of lies and illusions. We have, for the most part, succeeded in doing so. (In some instances, we have had to accede to an informant's request for anonymity.) In those few areas where it was impossible to ferret out the truth, we have indicated why. The question marks are as interesting as the exclamation points.

E. A., W. H., W. T.

Part One

ENTRAPMENT

Prologue

Santa Marta Acatitla Prison, Mexico. August 18, 1971.
6:35 P.M. A supercharged helicopter dips through a
misty rain into an interior courtyard where two waiting
prisoners race to climb aboard. Ten seconds later, it
rises over the thirty-foot wall in plain sight of the
astonished tower guards and flies off without a shot
being fired.

Friday morning, August 20. The front pages of most
major newspapers labeled it "The Jailbreak of the
Century." The stories disclosed that one of the two
"helifugitives" was convicted murderer Joel David
Kaplan, an American sugar and molasses millionaire
with a history of involvement in Caribbean politics, and
a nephew of the well-connected New York financier
Jacob M. Kaplan, whose nonprofit Kaplan Fund had
been exposed in 1965 as a secret CIA conduit.

A Reuter's dispatch quoted the helicopter escapee's

distinguished Mexican attorney, Victor Velasquez: "Kaplan was without doubt a member of the CIA, and only the CIA could have freed him."

The New York Times subsequently reported the same Mr. Velasquez as saying that he did not think the CIA had been involved at all "because they would not have waited nine years to get him out."

Kaplan's American attorney, the internationally famous Melvin Belli, claimed the CIA had nothing to do with it.

But *Time* magazine, referring to the escape as vintage "Mission Impossible," kept the CIA rumors alive.

And at a Washington dinner party, a high U.S. Intelligence officer, when asked what Kaplan's escape might mean to his agency, was reported to have replied: "It could be catastrophic!"

Newsweek added another contender to the confusion: the Mafia. "Far from being a U.S. agent, insiders argued Kaplan was a kingpin in the illicit drug trade and had been freed from prison by his friends in the underworld."

The underground press in the United States had this explanation of the jailing, if not the escape: Kaplan had remained in a Mexican jail for over nine years for his own safety, to avoid becoming one in a series of alleged "mysterious deaths" that had followed in the wake of the assassination of President John F. Kennedy.

Amid these conflicting rumors, the only clear truth was that no one in an official capacity knew who had engineered this James Bond-like escape or to where Joel Kaplan had disappeared.

What follows is a story so bizarre it would never be acceptable as fiction. The characters who wind through it are themselves so eccentric, so exotic, they challenge belief. To wit, and in no particular order: a defrocked Mexican priest who had swindled an orphanage; a Russian-born pornographer saved from a murder rap by the U.S. Secretary of State; a corpse that allegedly had its eyeballs changed; an Israeli spy with a withered right arm who ran a bordello in West Germany; a disappearing scientist with a secret formula to revolutionize the processing of sugar; an ex-Amos 'n Andy comedian turned illicit stock promoter; an ambitious skin-flick model with a voluptuous body and a penchant for taking off her expensive clothes in public; three world-famous attorneys; two Caribbean dictators of diametrically opposite political persuasion; and more, many more, all of whom were directly party to the plight of our hero, Joel David Kaplan, the most engaging eccentric of them all. It is, for all its oddities, a story of our times, an immorality play, a titanic struggle that became so consuming one might think the fate of the world hung in the balance.

Perhaps, in a way, it did. Perhaps this wild tale reflects our world too well. Perhaps the name of the game is Folly and Madness, and all of us, wittingly or not, are participants as well as spectators.

Such a game had become the essence of Joel Kaplan's life, though he was the most unlikely player imaginable. One might well begin by asking how a nice Jewish boy from a highly respected millionaire family could find himself in a Mexican jail convicted of murder.

How, indeed. . . .

1 The story begins ten years before the escape, on November 22, 1961. Alongside the old road that runs south from Mexico City to Cuernavaca, a road bloodied by ancient armies even before the Spanish conqueror Hernando Cortés pillaged the Aztec civilization in the sixteenth century, a pack of dogs of the village of Pueblo de Ajusco were yelping in a ravine cluttered with debris. Not until two young boys dispersed them with shouts and a few well-aimed stones was the ravine given any attention. What the boys saw jolted their innocence, a macabre sight right out of an old Hitchcock film: extending from a crude shallow grave that the dogs had pawed open, a chewed-up human foot lay exposed on the sod.

The boys sped off to tell their elders. Gradually, a crowd gathered to stand and watch. Too wary to dig, they patiently waited for the police. Why rush, after all? What could it be but a human body, obviously very dead and therefore of no use to anyone.

To the police, however, it was another matter, and they immediately dispatched Captain J. Jesús García a Jiménez, head of the Eighth Group for Homicide of the Secret Service. The captain had been waiting for this discovery for four days, ever since 5:15 in the evening of November 18th, when two patrolling officers of the

6

Federal Highway Police had spotted some abandoned clothes in a ditch along a lovers' lane called El Segundo Cantil. On closer inspection, they had found a jacket, shirt, trousers, and one shoe, all of them bloodied. In the pockets there were assorted personal items: a key to room 908 of the Continental Hilton Hotel, 603 pesos ($48.12 in U.S. exchange), and six canceled checks drawn on the account of the Paint Company of America and endorsed by its president, Luis Melchor Vidal, Jr.

Now, four days later, Captain Jiménez, arriving at the scene with several of his staff, uncovered the corpse from a "ditch about three meters in depth where a foot was to be seen, which foot was corroded and had lost its toes . . . a male corpse, his face covered with an undershirt, belly down, appearing to be dead not recently, having a temperature lower than the atmosphere."

They wasted no time bringing the body to the Mexico City morgue along the Calle de Niños Héroes where it was duly noted that four bullets had entered the body, three in the face, one in the upper chest.

It was immediately assumed that the corpse belonged to the bloody clothes of Luis M. Vidal, Jr. Now all that was needed was proper identification by two witnesses, after which a death certificate could be issued and a murder case initiated.

Captain Jiménez's visit to the Continental Hilton Hotel immediately uncovered one witness, a chambermaid named Sofia Trejo Orta, a thirty-eight-year-old spinster. Srta. Trejo testified that she had seen the occupant of room 908 on November 12th, "as he was seated on the fringe of the bed in shirtsleeves . . . he was phoning and spoke in English." Sofia Trejo was brought to the morgue where she viewed the body, then swore this was the same person she had seen in room 908.

A considerably more important witness was a hasty arrival from New York, the beautiful Teresa Carrasquillo, a dancer whom the police described as "wife of the man who, when living, was named Luis M. Vidal, Jr. . . . Catholic, born in Puerto Rico, residing at 465 West End Avenue, New York, N.Y." Teresa also viewed the corpse and identified it as her husband.

So, it appeared, the Secret Service, Eighth Group for Homicide, had its identification.

There were others, however, who were not so certain. Morgue workers, for example. Those who had seen the corpse described it as being between fifty-five and sixty years old; Vidal was thirty-eight. They described the body as far more Turkish than Latin in appearance. (In fact, they nicknamed it "El Turco.") Above all, it appeared to be far larger than the bloody clothes. Surely, ordinary common sense would require that the police try those clothes on the corpse when faced with such a discrepancy . . . and yet they never did.

What's more, intimates of Vidal knew his eyes were brown, yet Teresa Carrasquillo herself admitted that the corpse she identified had blue eyes. When later asked how she could explain such a contradiction, she suggested that "someone had changed his eyeballs." At the time, however, she made no mention of it.

None of these compromising factors appeared to bother the police. The clothes were not tried on, not one of all Vidal's numerous Mexico City acquaintances was summoned or came forward to view or identify the body, dental charts were not requested from Vidal's New York dentist, and the police insisted no fingerprints were possible because the finger tissue had been all but obliterated—surely highly suspicious in itself.

Still other observers took exception to the two women and their "positive identifications": the chambermaid, Sofia Trejo, who had entered the morgue in something less than a rational manner, became hysterical when she saw the body on a distant slab, then ran from the hall, a rabbit from a wolf. Even under more

8

propitious circumstances, one might wonder how a chambermaid would so clearly remember one guest from among hundreds seen ten days before and, by her own account, for no more than a few seconds.

And the tempestuous dancer whom the authorities acknowledged as the dead man's wife? How could the police be so certain of her actual identification of the corpse when she, too, went into a fit and fainted as she entered that macabre room?

If the police had any afterthoughts about further identification of the corpse, they had no opportunity to indulge them. Mrs. Vidal quickly recovered from her fainting spell and, with an efficiency unusual for a distraught widow, arranged for the overnight embalming of the corpse, its sealing in a moderately priced coffin, and its airfreight delivery to a funeral home in Brooklyn. There is no record of the coffin ever being opened for any purpose. Despite the proximity of the victim's friends, parents, and illustrious relatives, no rosary was said, no burial mass or funeral was held, and no graveyard ceremonies were performed. Subsequent attempts to inquire into the hasty funeral maneuvers proved futile: the Mexico City mortuary which transshipped Vidal's coffin to its final resting place reported that the several persons who had handled the burial arrangements were no longer in its employ and had left no forwarding addresses.

Very strange, the reader might well speculate.

Very strange, certain Mexican authorities eventually conceded. In fact, they refused to issue an official death certificate, so uncertain was this police "identification."

No death certificate, no official death—in Mexican law, a prerequisite to the disposition of all matters concerning the dead, including murder.

2

It is in the nature of investigating agencies to make the most of whatever they have at hand. For Captain Jesús García a Jiménez, if there was a certain flimsiness in the identification of the corpse, it did not appear to bother him. The law would take care of that, one way or another. This would not be the first time in his experience there were discrepancies in the evidence. Like any reasonable civil servant, he always followed the path of least resistance. After all, what were his choices at this point? He had a corpse and some bloody clothes with a name attached to them, and that vague but familiar pattern of unfolding testimony that linked the two. And since it was a matter concerning an American businessman, he knew enough to bend whichever way the wind would blow him. Inevitably, details would present themselves. He would be patient. And if he were lucky, he would eventually learn "where the treasure was buried."

At the moment, however, he had only the name— Luis Melchor Vidal, Jr. The woman claiming to be Vidal's wife had added nothing, and her hurried departure from Mexico City with the body seemed to indicate she never would.

In truth, the major knew only enough to worry him. Vidal. Was it Vidal? If so, why was he murdered?

If not, why was it made to seem so, or *not* seem so, depending on one's vantage point? And if Vidal had not been murdered, then where was he?

Who was Vidal? That question the major could answer with fair certainty.

Luis Melchor Vidal, Jr., was the son of a distinguished Spanish-Puerto Rican family. Vidal liked to brag that he was distantly related to Jacqueline Bouvier (then Kennedy), to the wealthy and prominent Gore family of Tennessee (which includes the distinguished former U.S. Senator from that state), and to the talented author and playwright who bore both these illustrious names. Vidal, Sr., had been born in Spain and had become a rich man whose friendships in Washington made him a power in the Caribbean, especially in the Dominican Republic where he had achieved an extraordinary intimacy with General Rafael Trujillo—who was godfather to Luis, Jr. The word around Washington was, if one wanted to do business with the Dominicans, the best approach was through Luis Vidal.

Luis Vidal, Jr., played in some of the same ponds as his father—but there the similarity ends. As is not uncommon, the pampered son preferred the more flamboyant style of the free-booting wheeler-dealer to any established occupation. Starting with U.S. Army Intelligence and graduating to odd jobs for the CIA, Luis clearly enjoyed the cutthroat game of intrigue. Although he was president of a firm called the Paint Company of America—as indicated by those canceled checks—the company was not listed in any standard business directories, nor did it manufacture or sell paint or any related products. The Paint Company of America was, perhaps, less a business than a kind of alter ego for its master, a front for a multitude of sins.

Charming, bright, formidable, Vidal's capacity for multiple involvements was phenomenal. He engaged in so many different types of operations that he was inevitably credited with doing a lot more. Vidal came to enjoy the myths about him, especially when they were good for business.

He was unquestionably big with women. Handsome, with large, romantic brown eyes, he ran around with all sorts; especially prostitutes. Luis even managed to profit from his pleasures, as in the business he set up in Mexico and the United States with girls he'd transported from Puerto Rico.

Vidal said he did not "approve" of drugs, but he found the drug business profitable and arranged a variety of shipments into the States from a sprawling network of dealers throughout the Caribbean. He made money; he spent money; he lost money. He was constantly covering bad checks with good ones; his bank account, like his life, was in constant flux. When Fidel Castro came to power, Vidal engaged in a thriving black market in Cuban pesos—as did so many others, although he became one of the most successful of the money venders.

Politics did not interest Vidal. He pictured himself as far too clever to engage in that sort of game. His was the politics of business, which neither knew nor respected ideology. He could deal with anyone, from a Rightist like his godfather Trujillo to a Leftist like Fidel. He spoke everybody's language and juggled their needs to fit his own.

His helter-skelter operations seemed to amuse Vidal, but they made everyone around him uneasy. The way he handled his gunrunning provides an example of his methods. He appeared to stop at nothing to make his bargains. He knew all the dealers who had access to weapons—all types of weapons, including B-24's from World War II and vintage Enfield rifles. Vidal would fly to a key contact city—Dallas, Miami, New Orleans— meet with Latin American revolutionaries in the afternoon and counterrevolutionaries at night, then sometimes sell both the same shipment of arms, presumably to let them fight it out through some victimized intermediary. In 1959, he began to take on jobs for the CIA, not as a regular operative but on a free-lance basis: if the CIA wanted guns delivered to forces with which they preferred not to deal directly, Vidal would handle their orders.

Vidal knew all too well the hypocrisy of government: wheels within wheels. This was Vidal's passion. It was as if he simply had to keep his head spinning with a hundred actions to feel normal and productive. He had a voracious appetite for food, money, women, adventure, and whiskey, although not necessarily in that order. His capacity, they say, was equal to his passion. But for all his talents and contacts, Vidal's pattern was far too reckless for survival—or so it appeared—despite all the times he managed to wriggle free.

Had he done so again? Or had one of his many rivals seen fit to dispose of him, leaving the fat "El Turco" as a calling card?

In the center of the puzzle was one man caught in a terrifying entrapment that would cost him nine years in prison and over a million dollars.

This was Joel David Kaplan.

3

On the morning of November 24, 1961, Joel
Kaplan began his day in the Hotel Bolívar,
Lima, Peru, with his breakfast coffee and the
local newspaper. It was the kind of simple activity he
enjoyed, sipping a fine cup of freshly ground Peruvian
coffee with the sensitivity of a connoisseur while satisfying his interest in the political and economic problems of the Latin American countries he frequented.

The phone interrupted his pleasure; a call from the
New York office of the Southwestern Sugar and Molasses Company, the family business of which he was
vice-president. Although he was in Peru to negotiate the
purchase of two warehouses for the storage of the company's molasses, the tension in his secretary's voice
immediately indicated other problems. With a stridency
not typical of her, she read him a report from New
York's Spanish-language press: a body, identified as
Luis Vidal, Jr., had been found in a ditch off the Mexico
City–Cuernavaca Highway, a few miles south of the
city.

When she had finished, Joel thanked her for the
call, then, quite calmly, returned to finish his breakfast.

This was his style: a quiet, subdued, unemotional
man. A private man who preferred breakfast in his

room to the sociability of the coffee shop downstairs. An unobtrusive, introverted man who disdained confrontations with strangers and the banality of small talk. A small man, 5′ 9″, a hundred and forty pounds, thirty-five years old, with a thin, sensitive face, light brown hair beginning to thin at the temples, casually if not carelessly dressed, a man who simply had no interest in clothes or any of the accoutrements of wealth. Indeed, he seemed more like a rural schoolteacher than a millionaire businessman.

Vidal was dead. Or so Joel was told. It was not entirely surprising. One does not swim with sharks without running the risk of being eaten.

Joel David Kaplan and Luis Vidal, Jr., were both first generation sons of self-made barons of the Caribbean sugar industry. Their fathers, successful buccaneers out of a more swashbuckling era of free enterprise, remained more friendly than competitive, often cooperating on deals. The exploitable riches of the Caribbean were so vast that there was more than enough for sharing—no matter how greedy or voracious the appetites of the parties involved.

In 1946, Joel got out of a landlocked tour of duty with the Navy and went to work for his father. During the ensuing years, he was constantly traveling in the Caribbean and Latin America, learning the sugar and molasses business the hard way—from the bottom up. It was an adventurous but seedy life. Given his ambivalent relationship with his father, it was impossible that it could be a completely satisfying existence. Abram Isaac Kaplan—or A. I. as he was called—was a self-made man whose idea for a self-made son was to throw him all the scut work and pay him peanuts for carrying it out—the paternal rationale being that if Joel didn't crack and could measure up under the strain, then someday, perhaps, the business would be his.

"Even when I was managing all of our Latin American operations," Joel recalled, "my father paid me what one would describe as less than executive wages; he rarely even paid my expenses."

To A. I., one did not pay or praise a son for fear of spoiling him.

Joel was constantly on the move, hopping from deal to deal, traveling often in the interior and usually on dusty, beat-up buses, rarely staying in a large city for more than a few days at a time, and then in second-rate hotels. It was a lonely life, and what leisure time Joel had was usually spent in solitary nights on bar stools in the Latin American equivalent of tenderloin bars, or in momentary, unrewarding alliances with available women.

Joel didn't crack, but he found other ways to compensate for the financial strain. "I liked the business. I was good at it, and I resolved to stick it out, no matter how tough my father made it for me. But even though I suppose I was some sort of an heir apparent, or wealthy man on paper, my father would never let me have any money.

"I suppose you could say I was a molasses czar without any sugar. I was ripe for anything that might come along."

Luis Vidal, Jr., came along.

The paths of the two men crossed, not unexpectedly, in their fathers' offices. Vidal Sr.'s company, Krajewsky-Pesant, was the largest sugar engineering and equipment supplier in Latin America. Its New York office was the headquarters, also, for the senior Vidal's extensive lobbying in the sensitive arena of sugar politics. "The old man had clear access to the White House —all the way up to Ike himself," Joel has said.

The two boss's sons became drinking partners, and then business partners. To Joel, who when they met was nearing thirty and feeling his isolation all the more acutely, the junior Vidal was a jet-setter of the low life, a person of interesting contacts, amusing dalliances, and potentially profitable and harmless deals on the dark side of the law.

Vidal in turn liked Joel's company, his trusting nature, his willingness to accept a new venture no matter how risky. And he surely had some satisfaction in knowing that, should he run into trouble—which was often enough—Joel would be there to help.

They were a strange pair, as different in looks as Rudolph Valentino and Dustin Hoffman, linked in a partnership of widely divergent activities—from drinking and women (even an abortive dalliance along the pornographic fringes of the movie business) to gunrunning. Joel was intrigued by them all, especially the gunrunning since it could be highly remunerative.

They had other ventures of a more grandiose nature. In 1961, the Year of the Corpse, Vidal sired what appeared to be a legitimate business, imposingly named Afratronics and Industry Corporation, and incorporated under the laws of the State of New York. Vidal was listed as a director and the offering brochure referred to him as a chemical engineer, a former U.S. Army Intelligence officer who had been awarded the Bronze Star, Silver Star, Distinguished Service Cross, and the Purple Heart. (He was, indeed, a chemical engineer.) A second director was Joel David Kaplan of 55 Fifth Avenue, New York, and a third was Robert A. Vogeler, a former executive of International Telephone and Telegraph.

The stated purpose of Afratronics was to exploit electronics, chemical engineering, and industrial development in emerging African countries. With prescience, the inclusion of Vogeler might have suggested to investors another purpose: Intelligence. For he was the same Robert A. Vogeler who was subsequently arrested and imprisoned for seventeen months in Hungary, charged with being a spy for the CIA.

Joel Kaplan was just another name on the Afratronics letterhead. He never met Vogeler. Vidal never called a board meeting, never issued a progress report. Afratronics' actual purpose remains a mystery. But what happened during the months between its formation and Luis Vidal's disappearance was less a mystery than an outright fraud.

Within months of its formation, Afratronics came under investigation by New York State Attorney General Louis Lefkowitz. By January of 1962, Lefkowitz had obtained a court order suspending the sale of the company's stock and he accused the firm's underwriter —Trinity Securities Corporation—of attempting to foist a $1.7 million stock swindle on the public.

Trinity Securities was a "paper company," incorporated for the sole purpose of underwriting the Afratronics stock issue. Its guiding light had been Warren Coleman, a black former actor and comedian whose professional credits had included the role of Kingfish on the "Amos 'n Andy" show and the part of Crown in the 1935 production of *Porgy and Bess*. Upon the issuance of the injunction, Coleman moved from his luxury East Side apartment, leaving no forwarding address. Later attempts to trace him proved futile.

With Coleman's departure, Trinity Securities also disappeared from its Wall Street offices at 40 Exchange Place. Not surprisingly, the firm left no forwarding address either.

The prospectus for the public stock offering had named four prominent African politicians—including the Honorable Jaja Wachuku, then Nigeria's Minister of Economics, and the Honorable Gabriel D'Arboussier, Senegal's Minister of Justice—as "development consultants." All four later stated they had never heard of Afratronics or of Luis Vidal, Jr. Each denied having given permission for the use of his name on the stock brochure. By this time, of course, the man who had made such free use of their names was also among the missing.

Joel Kaplan and Luis Vidal, Jr., were involved in one other publicly listed business: the American Sucrose Corporation, which was a model of probity by comparison with Afratronics. American Sucrose was a three-way partnership in which Joel was president, Vidal was treasurer, and one Dr. José Santos was vice-president. Santos was also the company's creative genius.

A Spaniard who was as unlucky in business as he was brilliant in chemistry, Santos had settled in the Dominican Republic in the 1950's. There he had developed several effective methods for dehydrating fruit. Unfortunately for Santos, the success of his business came to the attention of Trujillo. Exercising his own version of eminent domain, Trujillo acquired the business. (Quipped Joel: "The Generalissimo was a man who loved the land. If he wanted your land and couldn't buy it from you, he'd buy it from your widow.") Santos acquired a one-way ticket to Cuba where he went on to set up a thriving fruit dehydration factory. When the Castro government moved to nationalize it, Santos—an unbridled capitalist—fled to the United States. With him went the chemical formula of his greatest invention—a process that would allow sugar cane to remain in the fields for a considerable period after harvesting.

Vidal met Santos in the course of his travels and he talked the beleaguered chemist into the joint venture that was the American Sucrose Corporation. Together with Kaplan, they would put the secret formula to the test.

A plot of land suitable for the experiment was

readied in southeastern Mexico and preparations were proceeding apace when, in 1961, fate again intervened in Santos's life: one of his partners was reported murdered, and the other was charged with the crime.

4 One key to sorting out the real from the fantastic in Joel Kaplan's life is Cuba. Cuba is sugar. Cuba was where Joel's father, sailing four-masted sailing ships, first made his fortune in the years before World War I. Cuba was where, according to Joel's own account of Kaplan family history, his uncle Jack "looted" his father's molasses business during the 1920's, leaving Joel's uncle rich and his father broke. Jack Kaplan flatly denies the "looting" appellation, stating that he and his older brother parted over business differences and both got their fair share from the partnership. Whatever happened, there was no question of the bad blood that resulted—the two brothers did not speak to one another for almost thirty years.

Cuba remained the richest prize, the crown jewel of profits of the lush islands in the eastern seas off Central America. It retained that pivotal economic and political position in the Caribbean through the period of the Castro revolution, a status that was to be altered only when the Americans, at the dawn of the troubled decade of the 1960's, decided to cut Cuba off from the rest of the Western Hemisphere.

That important U.S. policy decision over Castro's Cuba was more than tangentially related to the key actors in this story. And it was a decision, one among so many, on which Joel Kaplan and his uncle Jack were to take bitterly opposed sides.

When Joel Kaplan first went to Cuba in the early 1950's, he came face to face with the most appalling poverty he had ever seen. He saw a fertile land rich in beauty and natural resources, yet its people lived in ignorance and squalor.

It piqued his curiosity, agitated his conscience, excited his hunger for involvement. Later, he was to recall the impact it made on him:

"I was there constantly, traveling around the island buying sugar, organizing the loading of ships. I spent most of my time in the provinces that tourists never saw, Oriente, Camaguey, Matanzas, Guantanamo. I saw people dying of starvation, living in huts with nothing in them. I cannot describe the baseness of it; there was so much of it, it was overwhelming. There were no jobs except for an occasional ship to load or a field to harvest. There was virtually no food and no possibility of help. Those who managed to survive had lived that way for generations, fathers and sons, always poor, and with no possible opportunity of self-betterment, and therefore no hope.

"I saw how they hated Batista and I thought how much he must hate them, all those millions who were his people, from whom he stole, whom he betrayed and exploited. There was one man who worked for me, a beautiful man, he came to me one morning and told me his wife was very sick and needed to go to a hospital. I went to his home and saw a filthy hut with no facilities, and a moaning woman of thirty-five who looked sixty. There was no place to take her, no hospital within 150 miles and no road to get her there. People lived, people died, and their government didn't care one way or another. I myself watched her die a few days later and cried for the waste of it, feeling a greater sadness than I'd ever known before. At the funeral, Batista's armed soldiers watched to be sure that no one showed any signs of having dangerous ideas.

"I could feel the Cuban anger—a pathetic anger since life seemed so hopeless. No one moved a finger to help them. The American companies made millions from Cuba and cared only about keeping things as they were, and Batista made millions in the process of obliging them."

In this, as in so many other of his viewpoints and sensitivities, Joel Kaplan was not his uncle's nephew, but neither was he his father's son. Joel had more than casual misgivings about his father's methods in Cuba. "My father paid the people cheap and worked them hard," Joel recalled bitterly. But Joel retained respect for his father—especially in comparison to his uncle: "My father was a straight businessman. Unlike my uncle, he never sought favors from the government. He didn't want any. He never cooperated with any government. My uncle went in the opposite direction."

Joel became haunted by his compassion and frustration. He became fluent in Spanish and, returning home, he frequented the cantinas of New York's Upper West Side where he would become involved in discussions with itinerant Latins. He was a strange bird to them, this friendly, professorial American concerned about the plight of their people, knowing just how far to go in an argument about politics, sensing their fear of the long ears of Batista, Trujillo, Nicaragua's Somoza, and their ilk. He learned from them and about them, for it was a decade of tremendous ferment.

Inevitably, then, Joel would rejoice at the overthrow of Fulgencio Batista on New Year's Day, 1959. The dynamic figures of Fidel Castro and Che Guevara intrigued him. He read everything he could find, made frequent trips to the island, and shared the hopes of the now spirited people. It was a time when he could wear his sympathies out in the open, a time when Fidel and Che were heroic figures who had liberated a starving people from oppression.

In the summer of 1959, Joel was visited in the Mexico City offices of the Southwestern Sugar and Molasses Company by two strangers who identified themselves as representatives of the new Cuban government. They wished to talk with him, suggesting that perhaps it would be wiser if they left the office, since there were others within earshot. Together, the three men crossed the street to a bar called the Tampico Club.

There they spoke for several hours, initially about the sugar and molasses business, then specifically about trade relations between the United States and Cuba. Joel impressed them with his knowledge as well as with his sympathy for the new Cuba, and they requested further conversations.

They met again during the following week, this time at the Hotel Regis near Joel's office. Other meetings followed. In time, Joel volunteered to prepare memoranda on the molasses business, the sugar trade, and other business conditions related to the sugar market, their mutual field of interest. According to Joel: "I was one of the few American businessmen in the Caribbean who was not opposed to them. I suppose I was the only one who knew the sugar and molasses business so well."

One night, after months of such meetings, the Cubans told Joel he could do them a favor. They wanted him to deliver some diplomatic documents to Peru— documents they could no longer deliver through normal channels because of adverse diplomatic conditions.

The Cubans placed a brown, oversized envelope, sealed with thick strips of tape, on the table at which the trio was sitting in the Tampico Club bar. Joel picked it up and put it in his briefcase. He was going to Peru the next week, anyway.

24

"I didn't ask what was in the envelope; it was none of my business, and they wouldn't have told me if I had asked. For all I know it was stuffed with blank paper just to see if I would deliver it as promised."

He reached Lima a few days later, checking in at the Hotel Bolívar. There, just as the Cubans had told him, he received a call from a Daniel Carlos who said he would be in the hotel bar with two books and a package, sitting at a rear table and smoking a cigar. Joel went down to meet him, carrying the envelope hidden inside a newspaper. He sat down with the man, exchanged a few words, then departed, leaving behind the newspaper-enfolded envelope.

Joel Kaplan, courier. It amused him, this minor league imitation of an Eric Ambler character. He enjoyed what he took to be the suavity of his style and the cool precision of the operation. He was, as a result, happy to do it again.

"Most of the people I gave such material to were rather sharply dressed. They were not too young. They were, like myself, not even Cubans."

He also made such deliveries to Ecuador. "I was called at my hotel and told to come to a park and sit on a bench by the statue of Simon Bolívar meeting San Martín. I sat there for about five minutes with the envelope enclosed in a newspaper. A man came limping along, sat down next to me, gave me the prearranged signal: 'I have exceedingly tight new shoes,' he said. I got up, again leaving the newspaper and envelope."

It was inevitable that Joel's activities in Vidal's gun-running operations would come up for discussion with the Cubans. It was not Joel, however, who raised the subject; he was operating on the premise that this was his private affair. About five or six months after their meetings began, the Cubans themselves brought it up. "They wanted to know all about it: how big the transactions were, where the arms were sent, who was bringing them in from the States. They said that they were more interested in certain arms not falling into the hands of certain people than in our general business dealings. They appeared to know about all the groups operating in the Caribbean; their Intelligence seemed excellent. They were particularly sensitive about what was going on in Guatemala, and asked me to tell them when Vidal planned to ship into there. I agreed.

"Then they asked me to divert such shipments."

Joel was wary, for it would mean crossing his partner. Arms consigned to one group would go to another, shifting from Right to Left, as it were. It took little imagination to see how such a diversion might prove dangerous to the dealer. Joel, however, agreed to take the risks. It wasn't long before he had to act on that promise.

A load of M-1 rifles and ammunition was to be flown to an abandoned air strip in southern Vera Cruz. The shipment, arranged by Vidal through contacts he kept secret from Joel, was to be collected by a Guatemalan group hostile to the Cubans.

Joel picked up the shipment and stored it in a nearby sugar mill. The following night, a twin-engine Beechcraft bumped down on the grass strip. Joel was waiting. He told the pilot there was no cargo on that night. "Then I warned him to get out or he might get arrested and his plane confiscated. He just turned tail and flew off into the sunset."

The shipment went the next day, to the group endorsed by the Cubans.

A few days later, back in Mexico City, Joel heard from Vidal. "He was very pissed off." Joel told Vidal that the shipment had been confiscated by the authorities and that the air strip could no longer be used because the situation had become too risky. Vidal did not believe him, but "there wasn't very much Vidal could do about it. After all, I was the man on the spot," Joel said.

Inevitably, Joel's relationship with Vidal had to suffer. "I think he may have had some idea eventually of my relations with the Cubans. The CIA had its sources too. One could figure that they told Vidal if he didn't already suspect it himself."

It was all very exciting and all very innocent—or so it appeared to Joel. For the first time in his jaded and dissolute existence, he felt he was making a contribution to the welfare of others, that he was acting on his convictions. Joel had been asked for advice and assistance by a people whom he admired, and he was flattered by their attention. He never considered himself to be an agent of a foreign power or even an operative, and certainly not a spy. Nor was his country at war with the Cubans. Joel was merely playing the Caribbean game according to the very same rules by which it had always been played, but this time, he was "on the side of the angels," as he chose to think.

Though he operated in maximum secrecy, Joel was not foolish enough to think he would go undiscovered. Where he was incredibly naïve was to think he could maintain such highly charged contacts with impunity.

Indeed, his punishment would turn out to be a crushing one.

5 It followed, then, that Joel would have mixed feelings on hearing of Vidal's murder. He finished his breakfast in that Lima hotel room, but not before the phone rang again, and again the call was from New York, about Vidal. This time, not only with the news, but with a warning.

The caller was Evsai Petrushansky, an acquaintance of Joel's, a Russian who had emigrated to the United States in 1936, a man with a colorful—perhaps too colorful—background. He professed to have been a U.S. Intelligence agent carrying on liaison with the Soviets during World War II, which was not unlikely in view of his Russian-language fluency. He also spoke fluent Hebrew, and was wont to tell acquaintances that he "not infrequently" carried out counterintelligence assignments for the Israeli secret service. After the war, he had turned to filmmaking, first as a bit actor specializing in roles that called for a menacing heavy with a foreign accent, eventually as a hard-core pornographer, churning out a series of skin flicks that were still making the rounds in 1961. In one of his films, an exotic creation called *Shangri La,* he starred his cousin Rita Nemirov, whose stage name was Bonnie Sharie.

It was Petrushansky, eagerly, who introduced Bonnie Sharie to Joel. From then on, he kept hustling

Joel to marry her. He was that way—the busybody, the fly on the arm that keeps coming back after being brushed off. Said Joel of him: "You couldn't keep him out of the house, he had to meet my mother, my father, everybody." Inevitably, he met Vidal, too, and, as usual, ingratiated himself. Petrushansky—on the periphery of everything and at the center of nothing.

With hindsight, Joel would say he had the innocence of a piranha.

Now the Russian was making pathetic noises on the telephone. "I don't like it at all," he was telling Joel in his heavily accented English. "It just doesn't sit right with me, you know?"

"What's that supposed to mean?" Joel was fishing. He never could tell what Petrushansky knew or did not know. It crossed his mind that the Russian had probably called to do some fishing on his own.

"Something has gone wrong down there!" Petrushansky was referring to reports from Mexico City, Joel knew, but it was all too vague for him.

Petrushansky urged Joel to come back at once, strongly implying that it would be a sad mistake if he didn't. Joel answered that he would return as soon as he had finished his work.

Although he had treated Petrushansky summarily, Joel was worried. The way it had happened, Petrushansky might have been one of the last to see Vidal alive.

That fateful week had begun on Tuesday, November 7th. Joel was in San Antonio, arranging for the sale of some huge steel plates from a dismantled molasses tank. He already had plans to meet Vidal in Mexico City the following week to implement Dr. Santos's experiments with his formula. But on that Tuesday, Vidal called from New York saying he was in bad trouble, but could not talk about it on the phone. He was afraid he might have to "disappear for a while." Could Joel meet him in Mexico City a few days early? Joel agreed to get there on the 9th, which pleased Vidal. Given his present circumstances, Vidal was unsure of his own timetable, but he would wire Joel of his arrival in Mexico City as soon as he could.

On the following day, Petrushansky suddenly showed up in San Antonio—not alone as he usually traveled, but with a man named Harry Kopelsohn whose distinguishing feature was a withered right arm. "A great soldier of Israel," Petrushansky described him, obviously to ingratiate him with Joel. An Intelligence agent, it later turned out, once part of the Israeli search brigade for runaway Nazis. As a sideline, Kopelsohn apparently ran a whorehouse in Frankfurt, Germany.

What were these two doing in San Antonio? Petrushansky, always vague, explained that he, too, had heard from Vidal in New York, that Vidal had claimed to be in some terrible trouble and wanted all of them to rendezvous with him in Mexico City.

It struck Joel as strange, though admittedly the sort of thing that happened frequently enough with Vidal and the Russian. He called his firm's representative in Mexico City, Luis deGaray Jaimes, telling him he was pushing forward his arrival date and would be traveling with two companions. He asked deGaray to meet their plane and secure a car, preferably a large sedan. Petrushansky then added to the mystery, producing a set of professionally made false papers he had secured in New York, one passport for each of them. Petrushansky was "Peter Green," Kopelsohn was "Earl Scott," and Joel was "Richard Albert Yates." Again, this was nothing vastly out of the ordinary in Joel's experience. He had used phony papers before when traveling on gunrunning deals. False papers made one that much more elusive to law enforcement agencies. It was the sort of hanky-panky Joel always enjoyed. But why was it necessary for this trip? The question rankled enough to lead Joel to duck his two companions and, making his way to the privacy of an isolated pay phone in the street, he called the Mexico City number of the Cuban Embassy and asked for a man named "Ruben" in the Economics Department. He knew no Ruben—it was the code name his Cuban contacts had told him to use "in an emergency." He quickly described the somewhat confusing turn of events. The Cubans, always interested in Vidal, suggested only that Joel go along with the flow of events, see what happened, and keep closely in touch.

The following day, November 9th, the three left for Mexico City and were met at the Mexico City International Airport by deGaray as planned. They checked into the El Diplomatico, a less centrally located hotel than Joel generally used, and spent the next two days waiting for Vidal, visiting bars, restaurants, and whorehouses, enriched by the Israeli's astonishing knowledge of the city.

Vidal arrived on Saturday, November 11th, and was met at the airport by Joel and deGaray. Vidal went through customs using his own name, which surprised Joel in light of the trouble he claimed to be in. Was he really intending to disappear? As Joel remembered it: "Vidal was friendly and garrulous and appeared pleased to see me. He did not seem at all nervous or worried about his problems, whatever they were."

DeGaray and Joel accompanied Vidal to the Continental Hilton, where he registered under his own name, volunteering to the desk clerk that he was going to stay for a week. Although Vidal again remarked that he was in trouble, and again, that he "might have to disappear for a while," his behavior was not that of a man seeking anonymity. He seemed to loiter in the lobby intentionally until his name had to be paged by an impatient bellboy waiting to escort him to his room. He again called attention to his presence by insisting that the valet service hurriedly press an absurdly patched pair of trousers with a large odd-colored piece of fabric sewn into the crotch, even troubling to make several trips downstairs to hasten the process.

There were stranger happenings that night. Vidal called Joel at the Hotel El Diplomatico, asking that he check him out of the Hilton and bring his suitcase to Kopelsohn's room. He gave no explanation for this maneuver, and, though it left him with no room for the night, he gave no hint of his plans. Joel obliged him, taking a taxi to the Hilton, paying the bill, then bringing the suitcase back to Kopelsohn's room where Petrushansky seemed eager to receive it. The Russian then told him that he was taking Vidal out for a while; Joel replied that he would wait up for them in order to return deGaray's Buick as promised. At 2:30 in the morning, Petrushansky showed up, giving only a cryptic explanation of the broken glass in one of the car's windows and saying nothing about some blood smears on the upholstery, which Joel was to learn about later.

"Petrushansky said there'd been a disagreement and Vidal had suffered a little accident," Joel remembers.

Joel could not sleep. He brooded over the comings and goings, sensing that he had been used, that he had been lured there to be used. Had there really been an accident? Was Vidal badly hurt? Where was he? Why had Petrushansky and Kopelsohn talked Hebrew in Joel's presence, knowing he couldn't understand it? Where had they all gone so furtively, leaving him to drink alone in the bar until 2:30 A.M?

Subsequently, he would piece the story together into a crazy jigsaw puzzle.

"The way I heard it, Vidal was whisked away that night through Kopelsohn's contacts with the Israeli underground. I'm told Kopelsohn bought a corpse at the University of Mexico Medical School—they ran into some difficulty and ended up with a corpse that was far from a dead ringer for Vidal—and he and Petrushansky drove it to Pueblo de Ajusco, where they pumped four bullets into it. They broke the window on de-

32

Garay's Buick and splattered blood on the upholstery. They must have beat in the corpse's face with a shovel to hide the fact that it didn't look much like Vidal. The fingers were mutilated to destroy any possibility of identifying prints. They couldn't even get Vidal's undershirt on the oversized body and ended up pulling it over the face.

"They dumped the body in that makeshift grave— Petrushansky probably dug it, since Kopelsohn only had one good arm—then returned to Mexico City with the messy Buick and turned it over to me."

Joel brooded for more than an hour after the return of the car. Then, around 4 A.M., he called the Cuban Embassy, which eventually put him through to "Ruben."

"You'd best disengage, and do it fast," Ruben instructed, after hearing Joel's account. "Otherwise, it might be too dangerous."

Joel immediately packed his bags, took a cab to the airport, and got on the first plane north to the Mexican border city of Nuevo Laredo. From there he took a bus to San Antonio and caught a flight on to New York.

The investigation conducted by the Mexican Secret Service leaves only a fragmentary picture of what happened during that telescoped period of time. One report quotes a Hotel El Diplomatico bellhop, Enrique Nuñez Puente, as saying that "these persons appeared to be nervous and were coming in and out of the hotel during the whole night, acting in a highly suspicious manner, even causing a comment in jest with the receptionist: 'One has to be careful of these individuals, they seem very suspicious and it seems as if they had killed someone as one of them has his shoes full of mud and his hands full of blood.' "

On Monday, Petrushansky rented a Corvair from Hertz. The one documented use he made of it was to drive Kopelsohn to the airport for his return to Germany. According to what Joel subsequently heard, Petrushansky made one other use of that Corvair. "He drove it back to the Mexico City–Cuernavaca Highway with the same suitcase Vidal had had me deliver to Kopelsohn's room on Saturday night. Petrushansky took some of the clothes and other identifying items and scattered them in the woods a few miles from the corpse." The Russian eventually returned to the Hotel El Diplomatico, leaving the car in the guests' parking lot.

On Tuesday morning, Petrushansky went down to the hotel parking lot, but the Corvair was gone. Unable to locate it anywhere in the hotel vicinity, Petrushansky was forced to take a taxi to the airport for his flight back to New York. What he apparently didn't know was that the Corvair was already at the airport. A Hertz airport employee, Nancy Hernandez, told the Secret Service that she discovered the vehicle parked illegally. Because Prime Minister Nehru of India was due to arrive for a state visit and large crowds were expected, she took a master key from the office and drove the car to the Hertz garage.

According to Miss Hernandez, a man giving the name Petrushansky came to the office a few hours later. "He was very nervous and troubled and walked to and fro when talking," her deposition read, "and asked if there was something found in the car, and the deponent answered that she did not know since she had not opened the trunk."

The man left without asking that she do so.

Several days later, the trunk of the Corvair was opened in preparation for a new rental. In it was a suitcase, which was routinely placed in the Hertz office to await claim by its owner. It was not until a month later that a Hertz executive inspected the suitcase, finding what were later identified as the personal effects of

Vidal. Among the effects, the police duly noted, was another absurdly patched pair of trousers.

Reflects Joel: "It was a bizarre weekend, all right. I suppose there will always be loose ends. For one thing, I was never able to find out who took that Corvair to the airport or why. And what was Vidal doing with two pair of pants with patches in the crotch?"

Quiet November days fluttered off the calendar; the corpse lay moldering in its nongrave; the bloodied clothes mildewed in the ravine. Finally, two patrolling officers of the Highway Police happened to be testing a friend's binoculars in that wooded area at twilight and chanced to catch sight of Vidal's bloody shoe—to be followed, four days later and a mile or two away, by the discovery of the rotting corpse.

On November 24th, a few days after the murdered and mutilated body had been found and "positively identified" as Vidal by his wife and a hotel chambermaid, a man using the name Luis Vidal, Jr., who answered to his description and matched the passport picture of Vidal, crossed the frontier into Guatemala. The entry was made from the Mexican border town of Tapachula. The Guatemalan immigration officer who passed the man through noted the U.S. passport number as 2938J2, which was indeed Vidal's.

"Something has gone wrong," Petrushansky had said to Joel on the phone to Peru.

6 For a man well into his sixties, Jacob Merrill Kaplan could move with remarkable vigor. On the morning of November 25, 1961, he left his town house on New York's Upper East Side and began his regular morning walk, over sixty blocks to his office at 55 Fifth Avenue, typically asserting his defiance of the elements by his refusal to wear a topcoat.

Upon his arrival, his first action was to instruct his secretary that he wanted the name of his nephew, Joel David Kaplan, titular vice-president of the Southwestern Sugar and Molasses Company, removed from his office door. As director of that company, J. M. Kaplan further instructed her that should Joel arrive or, perhaps, call to speak to him, permission was to be denied. The old man wanted no further contact with him.

The Kaplan history was repeating itself: three decades earlier, it had been Joel's father, Abram Isaac Kaplan, who had severed contact with this same man, though for totally different reasons. It was all part of a family saga suggestive of *The Brothers Karamazov,* with Jacob lacking none of the tyrannical Fyodor's sound and fury.

36

Uncle Jack, like his nephew Joel, is a man of many parts, though one must hastily add that there the similarity ends. Indeed, all of the parts are different.

J. M. Kaplan: multimillionaire, angel for leading political liberals, philanthropist, university benefactor, supporter of the arts, real estate magnate, newspaper publisher, and more, much more. Power and money breed myths, especially when the man is as complex as J. M. Kaplan.

According to his oldest daughter, Mrs. Joan Felice Davidson: "My father is a generous, socially minded man who is dedicated to giving his money and time to worthwhile causes and institutions."

According to his niece, Mrs. Judy Dowis, Joel's sister: "My uncle is a miserable skinflint."

According to Mrs. Susan Rosensteil, granddaughter of the celebrated founder of the Hebrew Tabernacle, Rabbi Edward Lissman, "Jack Kaplan was a hypocrite. He and Henry Kaplan joined my grandfather's congregation and for a while were active. Then, one day, they came to my grandfather and offered him a hundred and fifty thousand dollars to endorse a religious wine they were producing. It was during Prohibition, and he refused. As a result, the Kaplans stopped coming to the Tabernacle."

As Joel and Judy think of him, Jack Kaplan was also a man of many contradictions. Emotionally, he grew up hating the Establishment and its inequities, yet he became the classic tycoon, a man who lived by the accepted codes of entrenched power. He was as hungry for money as any of the capitalists he despised. He was as parsimonious as a Scrooge: Judy recalls that, at a time when he ran the Welch Grape Juice Company, his sole Christmas gift to the family was a single jar of grape jelly. Uneducated, he used his wealth and influence to associate himself with higher educational institutions—Brandeis University, the New School for

Social Research in New York—and he found special gratification in appointing their presidents.

There was grit and poverty in his history. He was born in Lowell, Massachusetts, on December 23, 1893, one of five children. Poverty, yes. The family grew up on a barren farm where Jacob recalls toting milk pails at the age of four, then hawking newspapers in Boston streets at seven, quitting high school at sixteen once his brother, A. I., began doing well in the molasses business.

Commented Joel: "My father, A. I., was a Russian immigrant who worked his way up from poverty and founded the Southwestern Sugar and Molasses Company. He was gracious enough to take his brother Jack in and make him a partner. But Uncle Jack showed his gratitude by taking what he could from my father, boring from within the company like a slimy mole. He got all he could out of my father's Cuban company, then started his own business in competition. For almost thirty years they seldom spoke to each other—not until my father was lying on his deathbed and my uncle came buttering him up with supplicating kindness. Not because of remorse, but to be appointed executor of my father's estate!"

As a family intimate once put it: "If it weren't for A. I., Jack would still be selling neckties."

J. M. Kaplan became a dynamically successful businessman. Nothing that had to do with money was alien to him. During the turbulent years of Prohibition, the family talk was that he was not adverse to engaging in a variety of bootlegging schemes. Molasses, of course, is highly fermentable, and J. M. Kaplan was in the molasses business. As Joel recalls, "There was common household talk that Uncle Jack and his brother Henry were involved in bootlegging with Meyer and Jake Lansky. Supposedly, alcohol was secreted in molasses shipments from Cuba. The ships would off-load in New Orleans where Customs officials were considered 'reasonable.' They liked to ship what they called 'half-and-half cargo'—half molasses, half alcohol. They made a lot of money in those days."

By the 1930's, Jack Kaplan had begun demonstrating a talent for the takeover and reorganization of sagging companies, which he would turn into profit-making ventures. Hearns Department Stores, for example, and then an extraordinary manipulation of the Welch Grape Juice Company. Jack had gone into the grape business with his younger brother, Henry. They ran a small outfit that tried to compete with Welch. Quick to see the inefficiency of the monolith, Kaplan eagerly challenged it, spurred by Welch's old-line WASP conservative contempt for the upstart Jew. Kaplan borrowed heavily and secretly bought up stock in the huge company, then marched into the Welch president's office and told him he was taking over the management. He was thought to be mad—until the annual meeting of stockholders wherein his holdings were revealed. A dramatic coup, and one that fascinated the business world only slightly less than what Kaplan did with Welch, for he was to turn the company into a tremendously successful operation, organizing over 1,600 grape growers in six states into a single co-operative that made the old Welch operation seem puny by comparison.

In the years following World War II, his vision expanded with his millions. He organized the J. M. Kaplan Fund. A nonprofit organization that by the early 1960's had grown to $15,000,000. Its stated intent was "to strengthen democracy at home and abroad through a program of general assistance, charitable, educational, scientific, and literary activities." A noble venture, to be sure, passing out thousands of tax-free dollars to educational institutions, promoting free Shakespeare in Central Park, saving such treasured landmarks as Carnegie Hall ("We stopped the bulldozers at the door!"), all to achieve prominence in that eminent world of millionaire patrons and politically oriented do-gooders, bringing him into the highest strata of the liberal establishment.

"My uncle's game was always to curry favors of important people," commented Joel. "My father was brutally tough in business. He exploited people. But he never sought political contacts to help make a deal."

In politics, which he loved, Jack Kaplan hitched his wagon to the Democratic party. Jack Kaplan did not always pick winners, though he definitely kept himself in the big leagues. In 1960, for example, when Hubert Humphrey was battling John F. Kennedy in the West Virginia primary, Humphrey was in serious financial trouble, so broke he could not even pay his motel bill. Jack Kaplan came through for his destitute friend.

Jack Kaplan had both friends and enemies in Washington—friends in the CIA and enemies in the IRS.

Though the Internal Revenue Service policing of tax-exempt foundations has traditionally been lax (at one point during the 1960's the Treasury Department had difficulty stating just how many such charitable foundations existed in the United States), there was one foundation the IRS attacked with unusual zeal and persistence, so flagrant were the alleged violations of the J. M. Kaplan Fund of New York City. Twice—in 1957 and again in 1958—investigations led the IRS office to recommend that the Fund be stripped of its tax exemption on the grounds that it was "never intended from its inception" to be used purely for charitable purposes, and, in fact, was operated by Kaplan as a tax-exempt "alter ego" for his general business dealings—including the use of tax-free funds under his control to acquire voting stock in companies he wished to take over.

The IRS charged the Fund with making loans to Kaplan's own family as well as to Kaplan-controlled corporations. In 1953, for example, the Fund advanced $400,000 to the Etched Products Corporation, which

40

was substantially owned by Kaplan's sister, Rose Nierenberg, and by his nephew and niece. IRS said the nature of the loan from the foundation was to "bail out" the privately owned business from its shaky position. "It would appear that the entire transaction was an integral part of Mr. Kaplan's effort to provide for his sister's and nephew's and niece's welfare."

These and other charges were sent to Washington by the IRS district office in New York in 1957 and in 1958.

In 1959, coincident with the rise of Castro, J. M. Kaplan's secret association with the CIA began.

In 1960, the IRS office in New York dramatically reversed its previous dogged position and announced that tax returns filed by the Kaplan Fund would be accepted as submitted. The office refused to elaborate on the reversal.

Though it has never before been publicly disclosed, in December, 1964, the IRS took two days of secret testimony from a former employee of J. M. Kaplan, a man who contributed numerous documents from Kaplan's private files to supplement the earlier charges.

In 1965, the watchdog committee hearings of Congressman Wright Patman of Texas tore the cover off the CIA-IRS secrecy over the Kaplan case, publicly denouncing the link and condemning the IRS for dragging its feet. Not only was the Fund a conduit for the CIA but, Patman alleged in public hearings, the CIA had intervened to stymie IRS investigations involving "a large possible tax liability as well as violations of Treasury regulations and abuse of the public trust, including self-dealing to the detriment of the Fund's stated charitable purposes."

Patman went on to charge that the IRS had been "trifling" with him in these serious questions by hinting that "I had better not touch this because it involves foreign operations of the CIA."

It was at this point that the feisty Texas Congressman was asked to attend a closed meeting with both IRS and CIA officials.

Patman emerged from that meeting to announce that his subcommittee would delve no further into the matter of the J. M. Kaplan Fund.

No one knows what went on behind those closed doors, but the result came to be labeled "The CIA Exemption" by Washington insiders.

J. M. Kaplan was obviously untouchable.

It was no secret in the family that Jack Kaplan did not hold his nephew Joel in high regard. To Jack, he was irresponsible, immoral, profligate, and a failure in everything he touched. There was nothing about Joel's life that he found commendable.

Nor was Joel's image enhanced by his associations with disreputable people and his continual involvement in dangerously illicit operations, the details of which Jack found appalling. Joel's miserable marriage to Petrushansky's niece was representative of all his weaknesses: lowlife, public brawling, nude movies, night clubs. Both A. I. and J. M. were revolted.

In Uncle Jack's view, Joel lived sinfully in an alien world. Since the elder Kaplan was not a man to seek changes or exercise the obligations that accompany compassion, his sternness was unrelenting. His judgmental posture remained unfailingly rigid.

The murder of Vidal, then, appeared to be the logical outgrowth of all Joel's sins. Jack had no difficulty envisioning the most sordid interpretations of his nephew's involvement. He was even to tell intimates that he suspected Joel's guilt.

The removal of Joel's name from the office door was only the beginning.

7 Joel was stunned. He had hurried back from Peru in confusion about his status, but he did not expect to be fired. One can only speculate on the scene: the millionaire vice-president of a thriving company, son of its recently deceased founder, walks into his office to find himself inexplicably fired by his uncle.

It was a bad beginning to his day.

He returned to the apartment at 215 East 79th Street that he shared with his wife, Bonnie, sharing little else with her. The place was as much a mess as it ever had been. No cleaning woman could keep up with Bonnie. A seldom-working professional model, she had a propensity for shedding clothes that were inordinately expensive to acquire. He had married her in 1956, entranced by her voluptuousness, by her shimmering blond hair, believing somehow that they could share a glamorous and exciting life together. It had been exciting, all right, but not in the way he had hoped. And he had experienced absolutely no glamour.

They made a most unlikely couple: Bonnie Sharie, the distant niece of Evsai Petrushansky, the pornographer, and Joel Kaplan, the sugar heir. It was a marriage spawned out of a desolate decade of Joel's roaming young life and the understandable desire of a

Brooklyn girl—on-the-make along the more sordid fringes of show business—to better her social and financial position. Their stormy nightclub-hopping marriage made them the favorite couple of the New York *Daily News*. Indeed, the pair provided interesting copy —replete with photos of Bonnie's ample bosom bursting out of flimsy nighties. *Daily News* deskmen had a field day with headlines like "WIFE WANTS SUGAR NOT MOLASSES" and "PIX OF BONNIE WEARING ZERO PROVES ZERO." They spent six years in a constant war, in and out of legal and nonlegal separations, divorce proceedings, reconciliations—all intermingled with veiled mutual threats of violence.

Joel despaired. He'd had another fruitless week for all the traveling he'd done. He poured himself a bourbon and speculated on what was apparently his total inability to choose decent partners. First Bonnie, then Vidal, both having come into his life at approximately the same time.

With that special sensitive foreboding that rides with bad times, he could feel he was heading for deep trouble, though he had not the slightest notion of how to avoid it. It was terribly undefined. He needed guidance and support, but he'd no idea where to turn.

It was the wrong moment for Evsai Petrushansky to turn up.

The Russian had already managed to declare his own involvement with the Vidal affair in an elaborate statement to inquiring reporters about how he knew absolutely nothing of what had happened in Mexico City. Yet it bothered him, or so he indicated to Joel. What was their legal status? What did the Mexican Government plan to do? He suggested to Joel that they go to Washington where, since Petrushansky had important friends in the FBI, all necessary information would be readily available to them.

And so they went, beginning a journey that would run second only to that of Phineas Fogg. In Washington, those "important friends in the FBI" proved to be too important (or too cautious) to return Petrushansky's calls. Joel nervously hopped a plane back to New York and went to see family attorney Louis Nizer, as recommended by his widowed mother, Mrs. Ray Kaplan. Nizer suggested that it might be a good idea if he left the country for a while—the south of France, perhaps, where the winter climate would be more agreeable.

Joel thanked him, but went the opposite route, taking the bus to Montreal, "where I had friends." No sooner had he arrived in the Canadian city than the Russian showed up. When Joel, more nervous than ever, decided to go to Paris, Petrushansky tagged along. "He told me he was just coming along for the ride." In Paris, Petrushansky rang up the Interpol office and blatantly asked if, by any chance, Joel Kaplan was wanted for murder in Mexico. Interpol replied that they knew nothing—or so said the Russian to Kaplan.

What Interpol did not yet know, or did not tell Petrushansky—or what Interpol *did* know and what Petrushansky did *not* tell Joel—was that the wheels of Mexican justice had been whirling at a furious pace, that a call had gone out to those nations of the world on diplomatic terms with Mexico, requesting the arrest of Kaplan, Petrushansky, and Earl Scott (Kopelsohn) for the homicide death of Luis Vidal, Jr.

8 It was a process that had begun the day after the corpse was found. Major Rafael Rocha Cordero of the Mexican Secret Service, the man who took over the case, did not think of himself as a lucky man, for everything in his life experience had been a struggle; yet when he eventually got around to looking back on the amazing progress he had made, he would have to chalk it up to good fortune—with a little help from whatever forces seemed to be controlling this affair.

On that day, November 23, 1961, the Major was presented with a man who turned out to be a first-hand witness to everything but the murder itself, a man who could sketch the entire affair with incriminating strokes, naming certain important names and leading the police to others. It all led to a lengthy deposition offered "by his own free will without pressure of any nature, for which he ratifies in all its parts and signs on the margin for the record."

His name was Luis deGaray Jaimes, and for nine years he had been the local representative of the Southwestern Sugar and Molasses Company. DeGaray's deposition read, in part:

. . . that the deponent [deGaray] borrowed a 1953 Buick from his uncle, which he then loaned to Mr. Kaplan who promised to phone him at his office when finished with its use . . . that after Kaplan's call late that night, the deponent went out of the office and shouted to the building's janitor who was asleep to bring him down in the elevator, then he taxied to the El Diplomatico and met with Kaplan, noticing thereupon the broken window, also blood stains sprinkled on the upholstery, even blood on the rear left wheel . . . that when asked about this, Mr. Kaplan did explain: "It is not possible, I did myself wash them off." . . . that Kaplan asked him a last favor that, by no means, was it to be known that he was in Mexico . . . that on Monday, November 13th, when he was at the office again, he received a telephone call from an unknown voice that literally said to him, in Spanish: "I am calling to remind you to forget that Mr. Kaplan was in Mexico in every facet of your imagination if you esteem your life and those of your family." A message that was repeated to him on the 16th, perhaps by the same voice.

Joel later said that he wasn't surprised at anything deGaray signed after the Mexicans finished with him. "They put him through two weeks of interrogation while shoving his head in a bucket of ice water till he felt he was drowning."

There was, however, another deposition, also attested to as a product of "his own free will," this one by Jorge Obregon Lima, janitor and superintendent of the building at 36 Balderas Street, Mexico City, which housed deGaray's office: "that the deponent [Obregon] was on duty as watchman on the night of November 12th-13th, and that there did not come in or out any person between midnight and six o'clock A.M."

If this compromised the integrity of deGaray's statement, it seemed not to bother the police. Nor did deGaray's subsequent retraction of at least part of his testimony, in fact, that he had received no threatening phone calls, either on Monday the 13th or at any subsequent date.

The police followed up deGaray's crucial deposition with the testimony of a variety of hotel employees at both the El Diplomatico and the Continental Hilton:

47

desk clerks, bellhops, valets, chambermaids, elevator operators, all of whom told of strange doings of three guests on the third floor, of their endless comings and goings during the long night of the 12th and how they left tracks of mud on the hotel carpet.

In due time, Kaplan's two compatriots were identified as Evsai Petrushansky ("a man who spoke with a thick Russian accent") and Earl Scott—Kopelsohn —("a silent man with a withered right arm"). So it was that, together with Joel Kaplan and Luis deGaray, they were named in the charge issued on December 12, 1961: "wherein the requirements of Article 16 of the Constitution are complied with in order to proceed in the criminal procedure against [the four] as presumptively responsible for the crimes of HOMICIDE AND CLANDESTINE BURIAL against the person who, while alive, was named Luis Melchor Vidal, Jr."

There was a foreboding irony to the denouement: deGaray, who had contributed the most to justify such an action, was promptly rewarded by being placed in prison at Coyoacan. It had been his misfortune to be the only one of the four who had remained in Mexico. Since it was months before the decision could be implemented, deGaray languished in jail while the three alleged killers roamed Europe, blithely ignorant of the charges against them.

Petrushansky left Joel in Paris and promptly took off for a visit with Harry Kopelsohn at his whorehouse in Frankfurt. Joel, still uncertain as to his status, called the G-2 agent in the Cuban Embassy. The agent knew about the case and he advised Joel to head for Prague. From there, the Cubans would fly him to sanctuary in Havana. Joel listened, then decided not to go underground. Instead, he flew to Spain.

Petrushansky, as it turned out, caught up with Kopelsohn at Wiesbaden. He spent several days there, then left just as Kopelsohn was about to become the central figure in a strange three-act drama.

Act 1: Immediately after the Russian's departure, Kopelsohn was arrested and jailed by German police for the "homicide death" of Luis Vidal, Jr. Mexico had requested extradition, and Kopelsohn was escorted to Paris on the first leg of the journey. There he got himself grounded by claiming it was a violation of his religious rights as an Orthodox Jew to force him to ride in any conveyance on the Sabbath.

Act 2: Dramatically, the Israeli Embassy in Paris immediately set out to get him released, their less-Orthodox diplomats feverishly working through the Sabbath to pull the right strings before sundown. Incredibly, they succeeded. Kopelsohn would not be extradited.

Act 3: The Israeli was about to be released into the charge of his government's Ambassador to France when there was a sudden halt in the proceedings. Apparently, the Mexican Attorney General, enraged over this violation of his request for extradition, had asked U.S. Attorney General Robert Kennedy for whatever assistance he could offer. Strangely, RFK obliged. He called the French Minister of Justice on behalf of the Mexican Government. As a result, Kopelsohn was flown to Mexico City where he was thrown into jail at Coyoacan, not a ten minute drive from the grave site at Pueblo de Ajusco.

Curtain.

Meanwhile, in Madrid, another drama began, this time with Joel as the protagonist. It would run for nine years.

This drama opened on a bright Sunday morning in the early Spring of 1962—over four months after the alleged murder of Luis Vidal, Jr.—as Joel Kaplan emerged from his Madrid hotel to be greeted by two officers of the Spanish Policia de Seguridad del Estado. Inside of ten minutes, he was seated across the desk of Captain Luis Pozo, Spain's Chief of Interpol.

A friendly man, as it turned out, who told Joel he was wanted for murder in Mexico. Since Spain and Mexico had not been on diplomatic terms for some years, no extradition treaty existed between them; however, he would have to be imprisoned, at least until Interpol could learn what disposition would be made of his case. Joel was allowed the equivalent of one phone call—in this instance, a telegram to the American Embassy pleading for assistance. He was escorted into prison, the first of many he would see, because of the American Embassy's failure to reply. And that, too, would be the first of many such failures.

After a week in prison, Joel was again brought to Captain Pozo who, this time, was looking more flustered than friendly.

"Orders have come down from the highest level of the Spanish Government," he said, "reversing the long-standing policy of estrangement between Mexico and Spain in this one instance."

Joel was to be extradited.

Two hours later, Kaplan was belted into a first-class seat on an Iberia jet en route to Mexico City, attended by Captain Pozo and an armed guard. And so it was that Joel crossed the Atlantic eating grapes and drinking champagne—a last supper at 30,000 feet before a most peculiar Calvary.

As the plane taxied to a halt at the Mexico City International Airport, Pozo made one last gesture of friendliness: he bowed to his prisoner with the grace of a nobleman.

"You are free to go, Señor Kaplan," he smiled. "Spain has no further interest in this affair."

The plane door swung open and Joel saw his welcoming committee: the Judiciales. And the Secret Service.

Over fifty Mexican law enforcement officials were standing at the end of the gangplank, two separate jurisdictions; rivals, as it turned out. Much to Joel's fascination, they suddenly began to fight over him. For more than fifteen minutes, he stood at the top of the ramp watching Mexico's finest in what might be best described as a barroom brawl. The Secret Service Commander, Major Rafael Rocha Cordero, urged them on, yelling instructions like a fighter's manager at ringside, until bruised and bleeding, the Judiciales declared themselves the losers and retreated in humiliation.

For all its zaniness, this opening display of Mexican law and order augured badly. Joel was pushed into a large sedan and taken, not to any headquarters as one might expect, but to the lonely rural road off the Mexico City–Cuernavaca Highway near Pueblo de Ajusco where the corpse had been found.

There, three burly offiers began to rough him up while the Major pumped questions and accusations at him. Why did Kaplan kill Vidal? Who helped him? Who was really behind it?

Joel denied everything, infuriating the Major, who pointed to the ditch where the grave had been dug, and continued to roar out his questions: Where was the money? Where was the $40,000 Vidal had brought with him? Joel cried out that he knew nothing about this, that he was innocent, completely innocent. In a rage, the Major ordered Joel thrown into the remnants of the shallow grave, shoving his face into the rocky soil. All they wanted was to get their hands on the money, Joel realized. He kept repeating, "I don't know, I don't know," his mind groping for some kind of explanation to stem the Major's fury. It went on for hours, terrifying him— he was afraid that they had actually taken him to the ditch to kill him. He lay in the dirt on his belly, trying to protect his loins from their savage kicks, his mouth full of sod as he struggled for breath. It was well into the night when he heard the harsh sound of barking

51

dogs nearby, and then, gradually, came the easing of blows.

They turned him over to the Judiciales at Coyoacan, who threw him into prison. Aching from the beating, he worried that they'd broken his hip and ribs. Joel was to say later, "I asked for a doctor but that was like asking for a bottle of champagne. They wouldn't even let me make a phone call."

Fearful of what they were going to do to him, confused about what they wanted of him, Joel kept thinking about the $40,000 the Major was after. It was obvious that the airport fight had been over that money. Someone, apparently, had suggested that Joel had gotten away with it.

"I've been curious for ten years," Joel said recently. "Who finally kept the $40,000?"

In time, the threats began again—intimidating words and vicious whacks on his legs with a heavy stick. They worked him over for days, pulling him out of his cell at night, never allowing him to sleep. They denied him food and water. They kept shouting at him until he could no longer understand their angry Spanish. They said they wanted most to find a way to get the others. Petrushansky in particular. They kept repeating his name, mispronouncing it terribly, telling Joel over and over how he could save himself if he would incriminate the others.

He couldn't help himself. They began to tell him a story of what had happened with Vidal, how the whole thing had been plotted by Petrushansky and the Israeli, how those two had taken Vidal out and shot him.

In the end, he gave them what they wanted, signing the deposition he was too weary to read. He wasn't particularly proud of it, but then again, he wasn't particularly proud of Petrushansky either.

Having signed the deposition, Joel was thrown into jail and left alone. Relieved, he abandoned his fears and planned his release. He was, after all, a wealthy

American and he had killed no one. He had but to secure competent counsel and get the wheels of justice properly oiled. It could only be a matter of time before the Mexicans would apologize and let him go.

There were, however, no apologies. Not then, not ever. And time became his enemy as days stretched into interminable months in which no wheels turned, and justice became the whim of unseen powers. Luis de-Garay, fellow defendant, also in the prison of Coyoacan, served ten miserable months before his Mexican attorney, Victor Velasquez, convinced the courts that there was insufficient evidence to convict him. Velasquez's case was based on one simple but stunning fact: the body of the alleged murder victim was never properly and legally identified; thus, according to Mexican law, no murder had been committed. DeGaray was ordered released. In the matter of Joel David Kaplan, however, the judge was not so lenient. Joel was found guilty, not of murder, but of "concealing evidence"; since he had already served a year, the judge authorized his release on a bond of 75,000 pesos.

It was now the spring of 1963. It seemed a decade since he had last seen Vidal or fought with his wife or walked freely in sunlight. As he collected his few belongings, he amused himself with iron-clad vows that he would never return to this town of defeat. He said good-bye to the warden and a few guards and inmates, then eagerly marched to the prison gate for a long-awaited taste of freedom.

Again, not freedom, but the Secret Service.

They were there waiting for him, just as they had been when he'd debarked from his flight from Spain. And there too was Major Rafael Rocha Cordero, just as he had been a year before.

They took him to headquarters and locked him up, adding another layer of silence to the illegality, and he sat incommunicado for over a week.

Then, Joel learned that if he wanted his freedom, he was going to pay for it, a fine round figure in the neighborhood of $200,000. In American cash, of course.

The source of this extortion was necessarily muddy. A quiet deal, as it were, relayed to him via a highly placed member of the Secret Service. It originated, Joel was told, through a lawyer whose father was an important figure in the Attorney General's office of the Federal District of Mexico.

And if he refused to pay? Ah, yes, the Major explained: Joel David Kaplan would be tried for the murder of Luis Vidal, Jr.

Your money or your life, the police were saying. A beautiful wrinkle, Joel thought. How does a man weigh these matters before an officer of the law, even if one is a rich man? What is a man's innocence worth in the precarious balance?

Joel decided to take the easy way out. He sent word to Uncle Jack he wanted $200,000 taken out of his multimillion dollar inheritance fund.

The answer came back: No. Joel Kaplan was a millionaire who could not buy his way out of jail.

It was obviously a time for counsel.

He was Edward Bobick, a New York attorney who now began the long-distance shuttling to arrange for Joel's freedom from jail. It was agreed that since Joel couldn't pay the bribe his only choice was to fight the case, for there appeared to be no way that even Mexican courts could prosecute on such flimsy premises.

That decision would cost Joel nine years and one million dollars of his family's money.

And yet, the decision to pursue justice in this matter was not an extraordinary one. Any lawyer worth the parchment of his law degree would have had to be amused at the government's case. Indeed, the courts had just liberated deGaray over the very same evidence. How could they acquit one and convict the other?

9 Evsai Petrushansky was undergoing a new experience, this one not of his own choice. On October 3, 1962, after Kaplan and deGaray had been in Mexico City prison cells for many months, Petrushansky suddenly found himself in the West Street Jail in New York City. He had been arrested by New York police for "possession of pornographic material," a charge his attorney, Leon Cooper, called a "phony rap" arranged by federal authorities who wanted Petrushansky held until the Mexican government could initiate extradition proceedings in the Vidal murder case. Despite his client's past history of pornographic filmmaking, Cooper was probably correct. The pornography charges were dropped after three days, and Petrushansky was immediately re-arrested by federal marshals on the Mexican writ.

Petrushansky was moved to the Federal House of Detention in New York, where he was held without bail pending extradition. That process was to consume two-and-a-half years of complicated legal maneuverings, the costs of which would be paid by Joel's mother, Mrs. Ray Kaplan. Apparently, Mrs. Kaplan felt her son's case to be so unalterably intertwined with Petrushansky's that, if one were liberated, freedom for the other would inevitably follow.

Cooper was to focus much of his fight against extradition on the flimsiness of the Mexican government's evidence in the Vidal murder case. His prodigious efforts on behalf of his client eventually produced a formal recantation by Joel Kaplan of his earlier affidavit to the Mexican police in which he had linked Petrushansky to Vidal's murder. In retracting that statement, Joel explained it had been extracted under duress. Cooper's most startling evidence was the testimony of two New York City businessmen with Mexican oil interests, William Suave and Homer Cobe. The two swore they had talked by long-distance telephone with Luis Vidal, Jr.—with whose voice they were familiar—in Mexico City on November 14, 1961—three days *after* his alleged murder. Cooper's third assault on the prosecution's case was the official document attesting that, on November 23, 1961, Luis Vidal, Jr., had crossed the Mexican border into Guatemala.

Astonishing—but apparently not convincing enough. The new evidence did not unduly impress the American courts, which consistently ruled against Petrushansky at every stage of the extradition hearings and throughout the subsequent appeals.

By the spring of 1965, Cooper had exhausted all legal avenues. The U.S. Court of Appeals had ruled against Petrushansky; the U.S. Supreme Court had refused to intervene. The green light was finally flashing for the filmmaker's removal to Mexico.

At that final minute of the eleventh hour, no less a personage than Secretary of State Dean Rusk entered the case on the side of the skin-flick *artiste*. The law did provide that the Secretary of State, at his own discretion, could intervene on behalf of American citizens and refuse to deliver them into the hands of foreign courts. But even Cooper, dedicated as he was, could hardly have hoped for, much less expected, such a *deus ex machina*.

On April 16, 1965, Dean Rusk and Leon Cooper met

for forty-five minutes in a closed-door session. That afternoon, a State Department courier delivered a letter to Attorney General Nicholas Katzenbach that read in part: "Bearing in mind that under Article IV of the Extradition Treaty of 1899, a contracting party is not obligated to surrender one of its citizens, the Secretary of State has decided to decline the surrender of this United States citizen." That same day, the Attorney General's office authorized Robert Morgenthau, U.S. Attorney for the Southern District of New York, to "take the necessary steps to terminate this litigation and to have Petrushansky released from custody."

Petrushansky was free. The reasons for the unique accessibility of Dean Rusk and for his countermanding decision have never been revealed. The only thing clear is that a powerful hand had opened Dean Rusk's door.

Harry Kopelsohn had friends in Mexico City. Important friends, as it turned out.

They belonged to the official family of the Israeli Embassy in Mexico City, and they used this to pressure the Mexican Government for a prompt trial, to see to it that their national had adequate counsel. The trial was unusually prompt for Mexico. And the defense somehow succeeded in convincing the three-judge panel that this was not really Earl Scott but an itinerant merchant from Tel Aviv named Haim Kopelsohn who knew nothing of such matters as murder. Observes Joel wryly, "The judges seemed to believe the testimony that Kopelsohn could not be Scott because one smoked cigarettes and the other smoked a pipe."

An acquittal was promptly handed down.

But in doing so, the judges supported the argument in defense of deGaray: "Since the body supposedly identified as that of Luis Vidal, Jr., had not been fully identified," they solemnly declared, *"there can be no crime to pursue."*

No crime? Then there could be no criminal.

What, then, was Joel Kaplan doing in jail?

The Mexican press reveled in this little paradox, running articles predicting that the Kopelsohn decision must surely mean that the release of Joel Kaplan was imminent.

The judges hastily reversed their opinion. It was not the body of the deceased, they clarified, but "the person of the accused, Haim Kopelsohn, that had not been properly identified."

With that deft about-face, Joel remained on the hook.

Kopelsohn, however, was not out of the woods since the Mexican authorities refused him an exit visa.

"The law," he sighed, raising his good left arm, "is like a feather in the wind."

Once again, Kopelsohn's compatriots came to his aid. Members of the Jewish community in Mexico City arranged with the Israeli Nazi-hunting underground to smuggle him to Guatemala. From there, he had no trouble finding his way back to Germany and his former occupations.

The departure of Kopelsohn left only one man accused of the same crime on the same evidence.

Of the three defendants, he was the man with the greatest wealth and the best contacts. In the annals of Mexican justice, it is difficult to find a case in which such a man of means in comparable circumstances would even stand trial.

Yet Joel Kaplan did. He was on the threshold of a trial that would boggle the minds of those who studied it, a trial that was not a trial, with unseen judges not even fully impaneled, no jury, no court schedule, no cross-examination, and no sense of order or chronology.

10

"There was power and money working to get me out of jail," said Joel Kaplan, "but there was even more power and money working to keep me in!"

Whose power? Whose money?

"I know that my Uncle Jack spent no money to get me out. I don't know how much he may have spent to keep me in."

There was a bitter family history behind Joel's anger against his uncle, and the frustrations of his plight served only to exacerbate them. Joel was convinced there was no limit to the man's capacity to cultivate influence. Joel himself had seen much of this demonstrated in the elder Kaplan's offices at 55 Fifth Avenue when leading members of the Democratic Party hierarchy paraded through the old man's inner sanctum like poor relatives begging for a handout. Why then wasn't he using them in his nephew's behalf? Why wasn't his uncle making phone calls to private numbers of powerful White House aides? Joel thought he knew the answer to that: the old family feud.

There were also reasons related to money—lots of money—for Joel to think his uncle preferred him to remain conveniently in jail. There was an inheritance of some $7.5 million, which was supposed to be shared equally among three beneficiaries—Joel, his sister, Judy, and his brother, Ezra. Joel's uncle had control of the money and none, as yet, had been distributed to the heirs. Joel was to say later, "I figured I'd never see my money as long as I remained behind bars in Mexico."

Joel also believed there were political reasons that might make his uncle prefer to see him sit in jail. And as time passed and the months were strung into years, Joel saw these political reasons as paramount.

At the center was the politics of sugar.

Sugar. The Caribbean. Cuba. The CIA.

Had Joel been playing too many tricky games in his uncle's ballpark?

Certainly, J. M. Kaplan was deeply involved in the making of U.S. sugar policy in the late 1950's and early 1960's. Certainly, he was close to the CIA. And certainly, the key issue in sugar politics was Castro's Cuba.

One Washington rumor, perhaps apocryphal but persistent nonetheless, is indicative of the power-broker role attributed to Kaplan. After Fidel came to power in January, 1959, it is rumored that the elder Kaplan was informally sought out by the U.S. Government as an expert in Caribbean affairs. As the story goes, Jack Kaplan was to go to Havana to take a bearing on Castro's political persuasion. How far would the new Cuban leader go to do business with America? Kaplan was to offer Fidel a deal beneficial to Cuba. It would also have benefited Kaplan. Had Castro agreed to the proposal, Kaplan would have pulled off an extraordinary coup for American sugar interests and for himself, and Fidel would have been considered "safe" to deal with. Castro, however, wasn't making such deals. Knowledgeable government sources say that Jack Kaplan's negative impression was influential in the formulation of Washington's intractable attitude toward Castro.

United States relationships with Cuba began a process of disintegration shortly thereafter.

If the politics of the Caribbean were especially complicated during this period, so too were the politics within the CIA. For almost a decade, an internal tug-of-war had been going on between the agency's "liberal" and "conservative" wings. The conservatives—hardcore hangers-on from World War II counterintelligence, old-line OSS types—preferred using guns to offering butter in the effort to convince other nations to cooperate with American policy. The liberals were the new boys—Ivy League sophisticates, Wall Street lawyers, university professors—who opted for more manipulative, inventive, and quasi-democratic means to achieve U.S. ends. By the late 1950's, this liberal side had prevailed within the agency and a new American intelligence stratagem had been initiated.

Eschewing the brute espionage and unilateral support of right-wing military dictatorships favored by the hard-liners, the liberals chose more flexible covert operations. In the emerging nations of the Third World, they argued, change was inevitable. To protect American interests, correct strategy would entail selecting and supporting the more moderate forces of the anti-Communist left that were seeking change in those nations. Clandestine support, lest it appear that America was interfering in the internal affairs of other countries, or lest politically unsophisticated right-wingers in Congress set up a howl. Thus was born the policy of supporting moderate centrist and socialist parties, the aim being to outflank the extreme left. Such regimes could be counted on to effect enough change to forestall revolution, but not enough to threaten American interests—political and economic.

The necessity for covert operations led to the necessity for conduits for CIA funds, and here the good offices of millionaire liberal Americans such as J. M.

61

Kaplan came into play. It was good that the CIA manipulate effectively; it was bad that it mangle openly. Thus, most of the money the CIA secretly ran through the Kaplan Fund was earmarked to support "safe" social democratic or socialist alternatives to communist or extreme and uncooperative socialist regimes.

Sometime during this critical period in Caribbean politics—between 1959 and 1960—while Joel was working on behalf of Castro, Jacob M. Kaplan allowed his $20 million nonprofit Fund to serve secretly as a conduit for the CIA. One principal recipient of these monies was the CIA-dominated Institute of International Labor Research. Through it, hundreds of agents would fan out into the Caribbean, posing as sociologists, students, consultants.

During this same period, J. M. Kaplan became friendly with the famed old Socialist Norman Thomas, who subsequently introduced him to the new Dominican Republic President, Juan Bosch. A fast friendship developed and it lent Kaplan the reputation of being Bosch's personal emissary in the United States. But the Institute's secretary-treasurer, Sasha Volman—an old-line Rumanian anti-Communist—began muddying up these liberal waters, creating typical counterrevolutionary havoc (with CIA funds) until Kaplan was led to believe that Bosch's regime had been infiltrated by extreme leftists. Within months of taking office, Bosch was ousted by a military coup and was replaced by right-winger Juan Balaguer, who immediately put Sasha Volman on his staff.

Although the Kaplan Fund has been publicly revealed to have served as a CIA conduit, J. M. Kaplan's role in determining U.S. policy in the Caribbean—and especially toward Cuba—is still shrouded in classified documents. Intelligence considerations aside, no American administration would likely make an irreversible decision about so critical an area as Cuba without first at least consulting those American businessmen most affected. And Kaplan's holdings in the Caribbean were extensive. With the decision taken, however, the Cuba file passed back into the hands of the CIA's hard-liners who, through such open debacles as the Bay of Pigs, would attempt to bring Cuba into line the old-fashioned way.

· Concurrent with the fateful American decision over Cuba, J. M. Kaplan moved to shift the bulk of his Caribbean business operations to the Dominican Republic. At about the same time, the CIA, through the Kaplan Fund, began feeding large sums of money to the groups it was supporting in that island nation.

The Bay of Pigs came and went; the Cuban Missile Crisis followed; periodically, rumors of anti-Castro Cuban insurgents on the Pearl of the Antilles flared and then died out. And still, Castro remained in power, and the possibility of a return to the enormously profitable sugar dealings with Cuba faded, at least for the foreseeable future. In 1963, J. M. Kaplan sold out his family's long-standing interests in the Caribbean to the Hawaiian sugar oligarchy, C. Brewer and Company, giving that firm a virtual monopoly over the molasses business.

The years between Castro's takeover and Joel Kaplan's arrest, then, were years of extreme political antagonism between uncle and nephew. They had chosen sides, and the sides were totally at odds. Later, sitting in prison, Joel would see himself as having been a thorn in the old man's side—the "pesky nephew"— flitting around the edges of all those delicate power plays. Did the CIA put Joel out of circulation? Had his uncle agreed to that?

Joel couldn't answer such questions. All he could do was sit in a Mexican jail, in rage and confusion, awaiting a trial that never seemed to begin for him.

DeGaray was back at work. Kopelsohn was gone. Petrushansky was free.

And Vidal? Where the devil was Vidal?

Joel alternately scowled and laughed at the joke that Vidal was coming back to Mexico City to testify against him at the trial.

Part Two

TRIAL AND ERROR

Two

11 The Kafkaesque trial of Joel David Kaplan was to be preceded by a game of judicial musical chairs. The judge who had convicted the prisoner at Coyoacan for "concealing evidence" and then set him free on a judgment of a mere 75,000 pesos found himself in extremely hot water barely two days afterward. A representative of the Attorney General confronted him in his office and demanded all files relating to the case. The judge quite legitimately questioned this request, but instead of an answer there was a threat to have him removed from the bench. The judge was bothered as much by his confusions as by the threats. Why? Had he been too severe or too lenient, he wished to know. He was informed that the case was to be reopened by a judge in another jurisdiction. The conclusions had to be rewritten to frame another indictment. The charge was to be murder.

A second judge reviewed the evidence and was astounded by the obvious breach of the legal process. Not only was the evidence inadequate for any such indictment, but the defendant "was being subjected to a violation of the law as it applied to double jeopardy." A third judge, succeeding him on the case, was equally appalled. He, too, reviewed the evidence of the first trial and then excused himself from further involvement. Concurring with the initial verdict and aware that the government was arbitrarily setting that verdict aside, the judge could conclude only that the authorities wished to preempt a legal decision. If so, he wanted no part of it.

The case was then brought to the First Penal Court, where three more judges would be involved. They reviewed the evidence for three months; then, one by one, they, too, excused themselves.

And so it went, bouncing around from one court to another for a full year—a case in search of a judge. But apparently no honest judge would touch it. Nor would any venture to comment on why. There were others, also judges, who sent word to the prisoner whose case they were likely to try, indicating their sympathy for his plight, suggesting that they could possibly arrange for his release—though at considerable risk to themselves. If the prisoner could promise $20,000—half in advance —proceedings would immediately be initiated in his behalf.

Joel paid, beginning a tedious road he paved with his own gold. It was to lead nowhere. He paid, but nothing happened. "Too much pressure from above," the judges told him, but they kept the money.

Meanwhile, his life at the Coyoacan prison was palatable, at least on a temporary basis. He would go through many phases of prison life before he was through. For openers, though, let Joel himself describe his lot—as he did in this letter to his sister:

Dear Judy,
Thanks very much for your last couple of letters which I have been too lazy to answer. It was not for lack of time that I did not answer them because here all that we have is time. But a surplus of time creates inertia. And also as here nothing ever happens there is little to write about, even assuming that one had the ambition to write.

Being in jail has no advantages. One does not even save

money, because what one would normally spend on sensible things like women and whiskey now is all taken by the lawyers. Of course, the lawyers in turn spend it on women and whiskey so the economy in general is not affected.

The routine is simple. One gets up in the morning, or one doesn't, nobody seems to much care. One shaves and showers or one doesn't. Here again nobody seems to care. One goes downstairs and has breakfast which consists of a cup of *atole*. After breakfast is the morning formation to see who escaped during the night. That takes ten minutes. Then nothing. One sits. One reads. One plays dominoes. One walks. One sleeps. Then comes dinner. Four of us have formed a marching and chowder club and all our food is brought in from the outside. So we have whatever we want. Otherwise dinner consists of *frijoles*, *fideos*, and rice. Coffee. After dinner more of the morning's activities.

I share a cell with an ex-priest accused of emptying the treasury of a school of which he was the superintendent. It is a fantastic case which received a great deal of publicity here. He is a very nice fellow and will probably be released very soon.

Another member of our club is one of Mexico's leading surgeons accused of shooting his wife. He shot her four times with a .38 and she survived. Incredible marksmanship.

We have two servants who prepare our meals, clean our cells, do the laundry, etc. We pay them ten pesos a week. Other necessities like whiskey, women, etc., are taken care of through obliging guards. In prison everything can be bought. As we are distinguished prisoners we have various privileges.

But still it is no place to be. I do not recommend it. I am enclosing herein a very important letter which must be mailed from Miami. Please do me a great favor and put an airmail stamp on this letter and drop it in a mailbox somewhere. Will write again soon telling my adventures in more detail. Best regards to everybody.

Love,
Joel

In the fall of 1962, Joel was visited in Coyoacan by a well-dressed, middle-aged man of medium height and a pronounced European accent. He presented no card, identifying himself simply as "a friend from the Czech Embassy." He suggested that Joel employ a certain lawyer who had specific ideas on how to achieve his release.

The lawyer arrived several days later, handing Joel a handwritten note he had received from Cuba's Ambassador, Dr. Carlos Lechunga, asking that "special interest be taken in the matter of Joel Kaplan." The lawyer was an old hand around Mexico City and had had several experiences assisting prisoners at Coyoacan. He suggested that if Joel were suddenly to become ill, he might get to a doctor for a checkup—a doctor outside the prison. Since the medical staff at this prison hospital was known to be inadequate—Coyoacan was a prison for short-term inmates en route to other jurisdictions—this was not an unusual practice. He also suggested the trip be taken by jeep, a procedure he believed he could arrange; while in transit, Joel would be driven past the Czech Embassy where "a stranger" would be stationed to assist him inside. Once inside, of course, he would be safe, and arrangements could be made to escort him to sanctuary in Cuba.

The entire scheme was the work of the Cubans, but it could be implemented only by the Czechs because the new Cuban Embassy did not wish to jeopardize its delicate diplomatic ties with Mexico, by then the only Latin American country that permitted normal relations.

Joel soon found that the maneuvers suggested by his visitor were readily workable. He indicated severe headaches; a prison doctor examined him, concluded he needed further care, and suggested outside examination. And sure enough, there was a jeep, a driver, and an armed guard in escort, to take Joel to a specialist in Mexico City, several miles away.

But he never got to the Czech Embassy. Not more

than a mile from Coyoacan, in a scene that became a pathetic charade, the jeep broke down. "I was out in the streets with the guard waving at passing taxis like a New York theater-goer in the rain," he recalls. "My mind went racing with the possibilities. Could I slip off into the crowds? There were so many people around, the guard would neither shoot me nor even find me. But I was simply not ready at the time, I didn't have a dime with me, I had made no preparations. We were still miles from the Czech Embassy. Besides, it was all so sudden I rather suspected that perhaps this was just another phase of the same plan, that I was going to end up there by taxi instead."

But Joel was going nowhere—except back to Coyoacan. A few days later, the plan was reactivated, the appointment made, the jeep ride scheduled for the following day. This time Joel was prepared; he had money in his pockets and was ready to go.

"On that day, I was having lunch in the mess when two guards came, pulled me right out of there, and without any warning, transferred me to Lecumberri."

Lecumberri rises like a medieval castle in the heart of one of Mexico City's poorest districts. It houses all manner of prisoners who are awaiting trial, sentencing, or release. Since the legal processing of the inmates is supposed to take no longer than a year, there is a promise of transience; in reality, many are held for much longer—and everyone knows this is so.

On arrival, Joel was immediately thrown without explanation into the punishment block. He found himself alone in a large, completely empty room fronting on an open yard which was, of course, walled in. There wasn't a stick of furniture, so he stood around as the afternoon wore on. Nobody came. Noting a water pipe running down the wall, but without a faucet, he responded to his thirst by kicking at the pipe until it sprung a leak.

He had his drink, but the broken pipe flooded the room.

Somebody came.

"There appears to be a leak," Joel said, in water above his shoes. Since he was already in the punishment block, he did not see what else they could do to him. Indeed, they came to fix the leak and eventually placed a cot in the center of the room, which he now shared with a dozen or more rats who made so much noise scurrying about that Joel, tired as he was, had difficulty sleeping.

That cot was to be Joel's sole piece of furniture for four months, the punishment ward his home. Inevitably, the pressure got to him. He would wake up in the middle of the night screaming at the wretched condition of his existence—which was the more unnerving since outside the prison nothing appeared to be happening to resolve his case. He began to fear for his sanity. To save himself, he started conjuring up idyllic pictures of the gratifications to be found in a bottle of whiskey.

In July, Joel was moved into C Cell Block. There, he was returned to the living, demonstrated in this instance by his first drink of whiskey since he had left Coyoacan.

Never had he cherished anything more. In the years that followed, there would be only two things in his life that could match this craving: women and freedom.

He was fortunate in his connections, at least insofar as the whiskey and the women were concerned. But then, in Mexican prisons, a man with money and an appetite can usually find a supplier. In this instance, the defrocked priest with whom he had shared a cell at Coyoacan and who had since been released was able to visit often at Lecumberri, keeping the supply of drinking alcohol more than adequate—unless the prison authorities chose to cut it off.

Joel was a full year in Lecumberri before the government found a pair of judges in the Second Penal Court, and here, finally, the case remained for adjudication although the third regular member of this three-man panel refused to participate. If this exception created a problem, the government did not appear to be disturbed.

And so began the trial that was not a trial at all.

Joel, for one, could not understand or believe what was happening. "The whole process was unbearable since nothing seemed to happen from month to month. I don't think I've ever known such frustration. Every few months a judge would summon me and a hearing would be held. No courtroom, no attorneys, no adversary process, no judge, even. It wasn't a jury trial; in Mexico, jury trials are only for public servants accused of malfeasance. I would go to an office, a few barren desks in a small room. I'd sit down. A secretary or court clerk would ask a few questions. I'd answer. A secretary would read it back. I'd return to my cell. There was no cross examination. I was never permitted to confront witnesses who accused me. The only witnesses I so much as saw were the hotel bellboy at the Continental (I was seen removing Luis's luggage and paying the bill) and the chambermaid at the Hotel El Diplomatico (where I admitted staying). How did they link me to the crime? So far as I knew, they didn't. Nor did they include the evidence that Vidal had crossed the Guatemalan border ten days *after* his corpse was discovered. Most of the time I heard nothing. I didn't know what was happening. I had several lawyers coming and going. I believe they tried to help me, but they were based in New York, and I would sometimes think they'd forgotten all about me. They were treating my case like a routine corporate dispute where both parties are content to let the matter drag on endlessly."

"Prison life is tolerable only if you believe in your imminent release," Joel said, when asked how he survived. "You make the best of it. I had trouble eating the food at first and I'd get sick every once in a while. I suppose this had something to do with my mental state at the time; I definitely was having problems coping with my frustrations. Once when I got sick, however, it saved my life.

"It was in 1964, a year or so after I'd been shifted to Lecumberri. I came down with a fairly severe case of hepatitis and was placed in the hospital isolation ward. I was there for three months and when I came out, a guard told me that two Americans had gotten to him and bribed him to kill me. Knife, poison, anything feasible that made it look like suicide. In fact, I'd been so sick, the guard believed that someone else had tried to poison me. As time passed, however, he'd thought about it and decided against doing the job. He gave me a suicide note supposedly written by me. It was hand-printed, similar to the way I write at times. It said that I'd killed Vidal and was too depressed to go on living like this and all such nonsense. I gave the note to my mother.

"My lawyer, Edward Bobick, later told me that this was a CIA setup labeled the 'Halliburton Project.' I never found out why they called it that or what the project stood for. Actually I found it difficult to believe: why would they want to kill me? It was suggested that perhaps they thought I knew something terribly important. That, too, was a frustrating thought, because I didn't. Then I thought, it could be that I was serving time for precisely the same reason they were trying to kill me, and that was the most frustrating thought of all. I didn't know what it was I was supposed to know!"

Mrs. Ray Kaplan moved down to Mexico City to be near her son. Theirs had never been a close family, nor had her relationship with Joel been completely rewarding to either of them, though this had been changing for the better during the last few years. But the thought of his being jailed for a crime so heinous was horrifying to her. She believed in her son's innocence: she had heard all the reports, and as early as the summer of 1962, she heard the word that Joel was being victimized by "pressures from above."

She would sit still for none of this. She had been party to "pressures from above" for too many years not to know how to use them herself. And this was precisely why she had come to Mexico. To apply pressure to get her son cleared.

Ray Kaplan was a complex woman, fully capable of understanding the complexities of others. For all the difficult years of her marriage to A.I., who was twenty years her senior, she had loved her husband and stayed by him. During all those years she had also learned a great deal about Jack Kaplan and she had long since come to hate her brother-in-law.

"Doesn't he ever smile?" she was asked once.

"Certainly," Ray replied, "when he thinks something wicked."

Nonetheless, many months passed before she became fully convinced of Joel's grotesque hypothesis: that it was Jack who was keeping him in jail. Once convinced, she became a counterforce to her brother-in-law. She went to work on the dramatis personae of the trial—when she finally managed to find out who they were—and sought to pressure them with the evidence on Joel's side. She became something of a legal expert by the sheer weight of her confrontations with all the details surrounding the case, suffering through the anguish of every defeat, then rallying with doubled energies.

But when she heard about the attempt to kill her son, she became furious. She took the "suicide note" from Joel and marched immediately over to the American Embassy.

Ambassador Orville Freeman was sympathetic. It was, of course, easy to be sympathetic in such matters, especially since there was all-too-little he could do to help her. He did not have to remind Mrs. Kaplan that they were in a foreign country and must respect their host's implementation of law. Indeed, one had to assume that if her son were innocent—and the Ambassador did not suspect otherwise—he would surely be acquitted.

One of the Ambassador's assistants was not quite so certain. He was Sam Shapiro, one of a new breed of foreign service officials. His name alone suggests his uniqueness in a profession traditionally alien to Jews. Shapiro had twice been sent to special schools for advanced training in Spanish language and history. He was, therefore, a highly specialized member of the Embassy, having first served an apprenticeship at the consulate on the Mexican border at Nuevo Laredo.

His interest became aroused in the matter of Joel David Kaplan. A fellow American was in trouble and there was something terribly dubious about the way it was being handled—not only by Mexican law but also by the American Embassy. In fact, it appeared to him as though it was *not* being handled by the American Embassy. Shapiro had recently interviewed Sofia Trejo Orta, the chambermaid at the Continental Hilton who had sworn to the Mexican authorities that the battered corpse was the man she had seen in room 908. Srta. Trejo had voluntarily presented herself at the U.S. Embassy, and, with Catholic remorse, tremulously confessed that she had made such a deposition under pressure from authorities, that it did not seem fair to the victim currently in prison, whom she had read about in the paper.

Shapiro had not been particularly shocked by this: the police of most countries were always pressuring shaky witnesses into positive identifications. But when he was also confronted with the "suicide letter" and the news of the attempted murder, he began to take a good hard look.

For a time, no one seemed particularly perturbed by the persistence of his questions. Even the Ambassador seemed attentive. Shapiro went so far as to visit the prisoner at Lecumberri, if only to be sure he was being well treated. At the time, Kaplan was still in the hospital with hepatitis and could not be seen. Shapiro left a message that he would be available to come again when the prisoner had sufficiently recovered.

That visit, unfortunately, never took place. Suddenly, without any advance notification, the same Sam Shapiro who had twice received special training in Spanish, was transferred to the American Embassy in Seoul, Korea.

12 Joel's life in Lecumberri was a continuing conflict that might best be called "The Battle of the Bottle," a yo-yo life wherein the prison administration's permissiveness on whiskey varied with changing personnel or, more frequently, with the mood of the warden. Through it all, Joel was bounced from cell block to cell block.

His stay at Lecumberri began in a cell in which the previous inhabitant had been mysteriously stabbed to death. It was a cell with a history of disaster, a haunted cell as it were, from which no man was said to have emerged as healthy as he'd entered. Joel managed to survive this ordeal, principally because his friend the priest was a frequent visitor carrying with him an adequate supply of Bacardi. But if the rum made the ordeal easier to bear, it never impaired Joel's survival instincts. "No matter how much I drank, I still kept the light on at night," he was later to say of this period.

When he was moved to Cell Block D, a dry season began again. It was during this sojourn that he ended up in the prison hospital with the hepatitis attack that saved his life. On his recovery, a change in administration brought Joel to I Block, and a new lease on drinking. Prisoners in I Block had large, private cells which they were allowed to decorate. "I Block," said Joel, "was for the big wheels." And the big drinkers, as it turned out. Some mornings Joel would be too hung over to get up to "make the list" and report for roll call. On such days, he'd merely stick his feathery head out of his cell door and yell "Present!"

One of Joel's fellow inmates in I Block was a man of distinction, General Humberto Mariles, a former Olympic equestrian champion. General Mariles, an aristocrat of quick temper, had been incarcerated for taking too severe exception to the antics of another motorist who had pulled in front of his car on Mexico City's major boulevard. The General shot the offending driver. Mindful of General Mariles' background, the prison authorities had allowed him the free access of his manservant, who made daily trips to Cell Block I with large quantities of liquor and other necessities of life.

"Everything was fine until the liquor ended," Joel said.

That grim event took place when a prisoner ratted on their high life to the Chief of Vigilance, who reacted violently. "He booted General Mariles' manservant out on his ass," Joel said, and the indispensable aide was forever barred from the prison.

Joel Kaplan was not being completely ignored by the world outside Lecumberri. Curious journalists continued to turn up at the prison. One such was Pearl Gonzales, a transplanted American working for the English-language *News* of Mexico City. Mrs. Gonzales née Fishbein kept Joel's case alive with fiery articles, one of which recounted an interview she had with him in which he admitted to having been in on a "conspiracy hatched in New York to make it appear that Luis Vidal was killed in Mexico." Allegedly, Vidal's father had been a co-conspirator, and the scheme had been hatched after the younger Vidal had undergone a severe beating in New York at the hands of anti-Castro Cubans who'd been doublecrossed on gun deals. Joel later said, somewhat sheepishly, that he had made it all up "to give her a good story because she had been so nice."

Pearl became a loyal partisan, conveying messages and sundry articles in and out of the prison. Directing her considerable charm at the warden—who fancied himself a ladies' man—Mrs. Gonzales was able to gain entry to the prison outside of the normal Sunday visiting period.

Pearl Gonzales became so involved in the case that she even wrote to Joel's sister, Judy Dowis, asking her help. "Even the warden told me anyone with money could buy his way out and he never understood why Joel hasn't tried," she wrote. "He said it must be a political reason. Well, the talk among the prisoners is that it costs $80,000 to get out."

She didn't rest there. On a trip to New York, Pearl tried to get in to see J. M. Kaplan, her idea being to convince him to put up the money to get Joel out. Uncle Jack took a dim view of her overtures. In a letter to Joel dated December 8, 1967, the elder Kaplan wrote: "What do you think is behind this Mrs. Pearl Gonzales, or Pearl Fishbein, the sweet young thing from Brooklyn who is now domiciled in Mexico and has been up here for several days, persistently trying to see me personally? What can she want of me other than blue chips?"

Joel received very few visits from Americans in a realistic position to help. One such visit came when de Lessups Morrison, the former mayor of New Orleans and a Kennedy-style liberal, appeared unannounced on May 19, 1965. Morrison entered the prison via "judicial channels," which Joel took to mean he had the sanction of the U.S. Government. He was interested in the case, Morrison explained, because the Kaplan sugar firm had facilities in Louisiana. Although mentioning no specific steps, Morrison promised to try to help Joel.

Four days later, Joel read the depressing news. On May 23, the single-engine plane carrying Morrison had unaccountably run out of gas over Ciudad Victoria, Mexico, and plunged to earth. All aboard had been killed.

The only other visit of note was from the celebrated attorney Louis Nizer, who stopped off in the summer of 1968 on his way to the Mexican Film Festival at Acapulco. Nizer was accompanied by Jack Valenti, the former Lyndon Johnson aide whom Nizer, through his connections in the film industry, had helped become Hollywood's official spokesman. Louis Nizer was one of J. M. Kaplan's legal experts; his wife was close to Joel's mother, Ray. As Joel recalls it, the conversation was rather nebulous but was capped by Nizer's promise: "I'll have you out of here shortly."

Joel waited in vain. His sister, Judy Dowis, says Nizer once told her: "It won't hurt Joel to sit in jail for a while—he's been a very naughty boy." The same sentiment had been expressed previously by a partner in the Nizer law firm, Walter Beck. In September, 1964, Beck, accompanied by an interpreter, dropped into the office of the Procurador General of the Federal District in Mexico City and declared that he was representing J. M. Kaplan, uncle of the imprisoned Joel Kaplan. According to the then Procurador General, Román Lugo, and a Mexican attorney who was present, Beck proceeded to urge on behalf of his client that the law be strictly applied against Joel because the Kaplan nephew was an extremely dangerous person who had always, when free, engaged in all sorts of illicit business in the United States.

Román Lugo remembers that some five weeks later he received a letter from the Nizer office ratifying

Beck's assertion that he spoke for J. M. Kaplan. And, about three months after that, the Procurador General received a phone call from New York; the caller identified himself as J. M. Kaplan, and said he was personally prepared to furnish certifiable evidence of his nephew's illegal activities over a period of more than fifteen years. Román Lugo told the caller the same thing he had told Beck: that, in accordance with Mexican procedures, all evidence should be submitted directly to the judge who had the case under study.

No such additional information was ever submitted.

If visits from the powerful were few, visits from the helpful were frequent. Among Joel's regular callers was the defrocked priest, a man who, for money, could be exceedingly resourceful and unfailingly loyal. The priest knew a multitude of people and all were available for hire. It was through the priest that Joel met Irma.

Irma Vasquez Calderon is a small dark lady with thick cascading black hair and a rich throaty voice. A Guatemalan by birth, she is from a family that had played an active role in the political fight against that country's entrenched ruling class, then moved to Mexico while Irma was still a young girl.

She lived in Mexico City with her mother, who ran a boarding house. Most of the boarders were students, but one was the slight man Joel knew as "the priest." One day the priest asked Irma to visit Joel. She did, and thereafter became a constant visitor and, soon, his constant companion.

It could be said that Joel's survival in prison was, in large part, due to her.

What began as a relationship of convenience soon turned into romance. Irma came to visit regularly, cooked for him, brought him books, ministered to his special needs, made love to him.

82

Joel decided he wanted to marry her.

"It was a pathetic thing to marry in jail. There are times when circumstances leave one indifferent to such niceties, though. I insisted on marrying Irma because it made what little we could have together that much easier for both of us to handle. But I find it hard to believe that anything could be less gratifying for a woman. I thought about that a lot before the ceremony, the burdens I would be placing on this wonderful woman. Who knew if I could win my appeal before the Mexican Supreme Court? Whatever the assurances, who really knew? And if I had to serve all the years of the sentence, what kind of life would I be imposing on her? All she could say was that she loved me and she was willing to take her chances. She would joke about it, saying I was really a very good catch, for where else could she meet an American millionaire but in a Mexican prison."

Joel David Kaplan and Irma Vasquez Calderon were married on April 28, 1965, in his cell at Lecumberri Prison.

Irma's capacity to support him through all the following years in prison was nothing less than marvelous. There were no normal wifely pleasures for her— even their cohabitations were less than private. For, despite the civilized system of conjugal visits for which the Mexican penal system is fabled, the newlyweds found their practice of connubial rights as subject to ups and downs as was Joel's supply of drinking alcohol.

"In theory, you could only have conjugal visitations once a week; in practice, especially if you tipped a guard, it could be almost any time you wanted. But there was no consistency as to the location. In Lecumberri, Irma could come right to my cell; I'd ask my roommate to leave, lock the cell door from the inside, and there you were. But when I was moved to the prison at Santa Marta, you had to go to a special area in the prison basement set aside just for the purpose of intercourse. Everybody called it the "tunnel." It was an underground passageway with fifty rooms, twenty-five to each side of the corridor; each room had a bed, a toilet, and a bare light bulb hanging from the ceiling. It was always cold as hell down there—even in the summer. You could stay all night with a woman, but it was usually too cold to stay there much more than an hour."

Irma never complained, coming and going with a persistent loveliness that was far greater than he'd ever known in a woman even in circumstances of luxury. "I suppose one could say that I was maturing," Joel said. "I thought much about that: if I were to survive all those years, my memories of Lecumberri would not be completely horrible, for I had found Irma, and in the process, learned much about myself."

There began another enforced dry spell soon, this one of almost a year's duration. It was broken only once when Irma succeeded in making a deal with the Secretary of the Prison Director whereby she could bring in "three small bottles for Christmas"—no small achievement since everyone was being thoroughly searched on arrival and guards were ordered to scour the cells for hidden liquor. With the Secretary's help, Irma smuggled in three tiny bottles of rum—bottles of the kind distributed on airlines for individual drinks. Joel immediately went down to the rubble-strewn bowels of the prison to hide his prize amid dead rats and broken light bulbs. In an old shower room, literally carpeted with dead rats, Joel secreted the three precious bottles in a niche in the wall behind some old plastic shower curtains, promising himself not to open them until Christmas. On December 25, he spent the day in anxious anticipation, unable to get to his cache since the guards continually interfered with his privacy in a pathologically inspired search for Christmas contraband that even stretched to the bowels of the prison where Joel had made his stash. Late that night, Joel went down to the basement, fearful that they had located his Christmas cheer, then rejoiced in its presence . . . and there, among the stench of the rodent dead, he very discreetly drank his wassail, three little bottles, one at a gulp.

"It was my first real Christmas in prison," he noted.

It ended an extremely difficult year under a Jansenist warden whose prison policy was so prohibitive that visitors were forbidden to bring fresh fruit to the inmates—for someone had informed the Director that fruit could be distilled into alcohol.

After the New Year, a less puritanical regime began as a new assistant director arrived. He proved to be a man of the world, and of his word, too—which, of course, was given only in exchange for money.

"He called me into his office, saying he wanted to do what he could to make my stay happier. He asked me if I wanted to work. I replied that I didn't really care about that. He asked if I wanted privileges. 'You can have privileges without working' were his exact words, I recall. I said that I would like to receive 'presents' from Irma. He nodded, suggesting that she put them in her shirt.

"This is exactly what she did: she came to the prison all hump-stomached, and inside her shirt were four quarts of rum."

Meanwhile, Mrs. Ray Kaplan's passion about her son's case had become so intense that it frightened her friends. She had not been well since the death of her husband in 1959, and now she was driving herself unmercifully. Repeated trips between Mexico City and New York exhausted her, a condition aggravated by the frustrations of her meetings with J. M. Kaplan. Each time they met, she said, her suspicions were confirmed that he was, indeed, trying to keep Joel in prison.

She would frequently confide in a close friend in Mexico that she felt she was "going insane" over this. Ray was a sick elderly lady but she would rage fiercely about Jack, threatening to expose him, to tell all the dirt she claimed to know about his business manipulations, even to give out what she knew to Walter Winchell (with whom she was personally acquainted), claiming that "would blow the entire case sky high!" As Ray's friend (who insisted on anonymity) described her: "She used to walk the floor in my home all night long, back and forth, chain smoking with a terrible racking cough. She was a woman who desperately wanted to free her son but who was torn by some mysterious commitment to silence. She was just as much afraid of what would happen to him if he got out of prison as if he remained. I suppose that's understandable: she told me her son's case had to do with the Bay of Pigs thing."

Ray Kaplan found herself operating in the gray world of bribery and influence that had always offended her. She finally admitted to herself that it was, perhaps, wiser to deal for Joel's release than to fight for it. So she dealt, paying the so-called right people who would hopefully open doors. Sometime late in 1964, she thought it was at last all arranged. A passport had been secured for Joel, a plane ticket to New York was bought, a traveling suit and packed valise were waiting. She had a car ready for him at the prison gate. According to her friend, "Ray was never happier. She was suddenly walking on air. She couldn't tell me exactly what was going to happen, but I knew she had finally accomplished the release of her son."

Interestingly, she had also been warned to stay away from Joel at the airport, that this was the most dangerous time of exposure, a moment when innocent people sometimes catch a bullet meant for someone

86

else. She agreed to be cautious, though she actually felt defiant. She simply could not believe that anything so frightening could happen to them after all they'd been through.

Then it happened to her. That very night, she answered a knock at the door of her Mexico City apartment and two goons forced their way in. They slapped her around viciously, terrifyingly, leaving her bloodied and beaten on the floor.

The anticipated release never came. Nor did any explanations.

Mrs. Ray Kaplan recovered and continued to fight for her son, unintimidated by all the violence. In the end, she was broken by failure. She had spent well over $300,000, but, when she died in May, 1965, in New York City, Joel was no closer to his freedom than when she had begun. Her friends say that the cause of death was heartbreak and exhaustion.

13

On the day before Easter, 1967, a mysterious package that smelled of big news arrived at the San Francisco editorial offices of *Ramparts* magazine. It contained a half-inch thick pile of official documents relating to the marriage of Lucia Magana and Luis Vidal, Jr., on February 8, 1965, in the village of San Dionysio in the Central American nation of El Salvador. The wedding was newsworthy in that Luis Vidal had supposedly died fully three years before.

The documents were impressive: the formal record of the marriage ceremony, which had been performed by Alcalde Miguel A. Turcios in the Town Hall of San Dionysio at 9 A.M., February 8, 1965, and duly signed by the Alcalde; the official recording of the marriage by Daniel Mira, the Town Clerk; the formal witness by two citizens of San Dionysio, Julio Flores and Alvaro Lemus; the receipt for the civil wedding fee by the Bureau of Accounts of the Republic; the certification of the marriage documents by Juan Ferreior, head of the Political Office of the Departmental Governor of Usulután; the further authentication of all official signatories on the documents by Ramon Gonzalez Montalvo, Ambassador and Director of International Policy

88

of the Ministry of the Interior; another document recognizing the marriage as valid under the laws of Mexico, signed by Angel del Castillo, the Mexican Ambassador to El Salvador; a similar official certification from the groom's country, stamped with the seal of the United States Embassy and signed by the American Vice Consul in El Salvador.

Accompanying these documents was a marriage photograph of the happy couple. The groom looked remarkably like all extant photos of Luis Vidal.

There was no letter of explanation with the documents. The *Ramparts* editors, no strangers to paranoia, couldn't decide if they had a scoop or an entrapment. They suspected CIA involvement. A Spanish-speaking reporter, Peter Collier, was sent to El Salvador. At the appropriate government bureaus, he found no record of Luis Vidal having officially entered El Salvador. Still, there are many ways to cross the border, and many names to cross it under—for a price. Vidal, if alive, was not a man who would wish to be traced; but, after a several years' cooling-off period, he might consider it safe to marry in a remote interior village and use his own name.

Collier traveled into the interior, to Usulután, the county seat for San Dionysio. Searching the registry of vital statistics, he found nothing recorded. That would have been very inefficient of the CIA. Troubled, he probed deeper, proceeding to Santa Elena, which had been given as the home town of the supposed bride, Lucia Magana. "This is a town of about one hundred people," Collier reported. "Everyone knew each other, and as in all small Central American towns, there was an Alcalde and Clerk/Registrar, both of whom were quite old and knew everyone. But nobody—not the Alcalde, the Clerk, the Chief of Police—knew of a Magana family ever having lived in Santa Elena."

To eliminate every possibility, Collier visited San

Dionysio itself. "It was extremely inaccessible, about fifteen miles of dirt oxen trail," he said. "The town itself consisted of three or four buildings, with the usual sleepy administration. The Alcalde, Miguel Turcios, and the Clerk, Daniel Mira, whose signatures appear on the document of marriage, denied that the document was a true one." He consulted the book of records, which contained no such page number as noted on the document. That page had been ripped out.

What puzzled Collier, however, was that the Mayor and the Clerk did not disown their signatures. They merely shrugged. "I went back into Usulután and got the Governor, to whom the Alcalde and Clerk of San Dionysio are ultimately responsible. We went back, and he proceeded to ream them out. They admitted that they had signed the document—but that it was false. Neither of them could read. The way that official documents come into being is that schoolboys write at their direction, and then they laboriously scrawl their signatures."

The two officials told Collier and the Governor that a man calling himself "Jaime Garcia" (a name as common in Latin America as John Smith) had arrived in the village and bribed them to sign the document and stamp it with their official seal. He had also bribed the witnesses, they said. Jaime Garcia had then taken the document to the Governor, who verified the signatures while paying little heed to the contents. "And so it went," summed up Collier, "with one impressive signature testifying to the preceding, up the line to the Vice Consul of the United States himself."

The question remained: who was Jaime Garcia?

At the time, Collier discounted the possibility of CIA involvement and ventured that Garcia was "the shadowy character, friend and procurator to Joel Kaplan, known only as The Priest. This sort of thing is really right up his alley."

That particular who-did-it question remained un-answered until 1972, after Joel Kaplan's escape from prison. It was only then that Joel admitted Collier's guess had been correct.

On the priest's release from jail, Joel had begun paying his former roommate several hundred dollars a month to do "whatever might help." Displaying an un-usual aptitude for counterintelligence chicanery, the priest had traveled alone to the interior of El Salvador and performed what one presumes to have been his last marriage. The picture, Joel said, was not of Vidal, but of an employee of Southwestern Sugar and Mo-lasses in San Antonio who was a dead ringer for Vidal and who had obligingly posed for the priest's camera with his little woman.

This enterprising and artful attempt at forgery was the first of an incredible series of unsuccessful but inventive attempts on Joel's part to get out of jail—with or without permission.

The priest had first sent the documents and photo-graphs to Joel's new counsel, Victor Velasquez, the dis-tinguished Mexican constitutional lawyer who had suc-cessfully defended deGaray. *Ramparts* got seconds when Velasquez elected not to use such sensational evidence. Velasquez, convinced he had an airtight legal case for Joel's release, thought such anonymous evi-dence, whether genuine or not, was unnecessary.

Victor Velasquez embodied the best traditions of Mexican law and justice. He felt sure that his nation's legal system would not allow such a patent miscarriage of justice as the continued imprisonment of Joel Kaplan.

For Victor Velasquez, it was just the beginning of the most frustrating, bewildering, and, ultimately, disillusioning case of his long and illustrious career.

In Mexican jurisprudence, the name of Victor Velasquez is as respected as Clarence Darrow's in

America. At the time he took on Joel's case, Velasquez had served as defense attorney in eighty-five cases, securing eighty-three acquittals and two mistrials. Beyond that, he was a man with an impeccable reputation, a lawyer dedicated to the highest principles of the law. Then in his early seventies, Velasquez had had a brilliant career, and he was by no means retired.

The Kaplan case was first brought to Velasquez by Louis Nizer acting at the request of Joel's mother. Their professional relationship did not begin, however, until after Joel's trial had ended. Velasquez was to supervise the appeal.

Unlike Clarence Darrow, Velasquez was not oriented toward the politics of a case nor was he in tune with the political pressures that sometimes control judicial destiny. He confined his energies to strict matters of the law. Nothing else concerned him. In fact, all references to politics appeared to bore him. He was not even prepared to admit that the questions such references provoked were germane. Some likened his stance to that of a specialized technician with all the limitations of scope the term suggest.

A handsome man, with long silver hair swept back over his erectly held head, Velasquez maintained his office in his home—a richly appointed stucco house in Mexico City, expensively furnished in the grand aristocratic style he cherished—a warm, gracious home, replete with many antiques, books, paintings, tapestries, and statuary. Velasquez was a Renaissance man with an abiding faith in the law as the highest achievement of civilized man's power to govern himself. Indeed, one tended to believe in the innocence of his clients partially because of his involvement in their defense.

Señor Velasquez believed in their innocence as well, and this was never more thoroughly true than in the matter of Joel David Kaplan. As a result, no case

in his lengthy career would leave him so pained or so
baffled—or so ashamed.

By 1966, Velasquez felt he had cemented his appeal
so tightly the Mexican Supreme Court could not possibly fail to award an acquittal. Velasquez's central
point in the appeal was the same one he had used in
his earlier successful defense of deGaray: there was
no official death certificate. Mexican law clearly states
there can be no murder case without one, and further
provides that such certification can be issued only
after two witnesses have identified the corpse in sworn
depositions to police. In the case of the body found at
Pueblo de Ajusco, neither of the two witnesses identifying it as Vidal had been sufficiently convincing, and
no certificate of death was ever issued. Without it, more-
over, there could be no legal autopsy, and thus, testimony as to the cause of death would be inadmissible in
a court of law.

Since there was no legally authorized death certificate, Velasquez argued, legally, no murder had been
committed.

By the summer of 1967, there were 14,000 pages
of evidence in the case, and the files were constantly
growing, provoking longer and longer delays that added
more and more testimony—which, in turn, created
more delays.

Said Joel: "No one was going to read those 14,000
pages to decide my fate. They pretended to read, but
my fate was already decided."

As for Velasquez, he fumed at the preposterous
posture of the court, unable to understand how there
could be any legal doubt of his client's innocence. And
he wasn't alone. The Mexican press was raising many

of the same questions: "Why is it that such evidence as the following was accepted in our courts? . . . that the body in no way resembled Vidal? . . that the body found was never proved to be Vidal? Why wasn't the defense's allegation that Vidal was known to have gone to Guatemala investigated by the prosecution more thoroughly? Why was the fact Kaplan could prove extortion not recognized? Why didn't judges of the Second Penal Court protest against documents lost, documents presented without dates or proper witnesses?"

There were other questions, publicly expressed but never in print, relating to the complete failure of the American Embassy to come to the defendant's support. Indeed, even Victor Velasquez, who thought exclusively in terms of the law, was nonetheless moved to suggest a political conundrum: "Every country in the world intervenes in behalf of its citizens in a predicament like this—except the United States. . . . Yes, except for Joel Kaplan."

In September, 1967, almost six years after Luis Vidal, Jr., was "murdered," the Mexican Supreme Court handed down its decision on Joel Kaplan's appeal: Not Granted.

In the same week, Velasquez picked up *El Heraldo de Mexico* and read that Luis Vidal, Jr., had been seen alive in Havana.

94

14 In the fall of 1967, shortly after his appeal was denied, Joel Kaplan was transferred from the preventive detention prison of Lecumberri to the maximum security prison in Santa Marta Acatitla, some thirty miles east of Mexico City. It was a pleasant change, out of the stench of the city and into the clear air of the country.

Joel spent his first day at Acatitla in the New Arrivals Building taking psychiatric and adjustment tests, aptitude interviews, physical exams. On the second day, he stood in line with the other new arrivals while the Director called out the name of each man and read aloud his crime. When he got to Joel, he stopped.

"Kaplan?"

"Yes, sir."

"I want you to know that there are no special privileges here."

Not merely stated, Joel noted, but barked like one who knew everything there was to know about him. He felt his stomach drop, barely replying with another, "Yes, sir."

He was shuffling off to his cell assignment, brooding on the dreariness of his prospects, when a hand on his arm restrained him. The Director, he was told, wanted to see him.

More trouble, Joel speculated. Worse trouble, he was prepared to bet.

"Kaplan," the Director said, "there are no special privileges here . . . but certain arrangements can be made for a prisoner's comfort. I suggest you see the Assistant Director immediately."

A trap, Joel thought. They were going to trap him into a punishment situation.

The Assistant Director lured him in deeper, telling Joel that he had come to Santa Marta "very well recommended" from the Assistant Director at Lecumberri.

"What can we do for you?" asked the Assistant Director of Santa Marta on the recommendation of the Assistant Director of Lecumberri.

Joel shuddered. He took a deep breath and drew from his resources as a millionaire who was supposed to know leisure and the way of the good life:

"I would appreciate a comfortable place to live, my wife, Irma, and an occasional bottle to drink."

The list was brief enough, but it came to a sizable figure: 3000 pesos a month ($375). Joel consented to pay. A very enlightened administration, very reasonable, too, cheaper even than Lecumberri where he had paid 4000 pesos for the same privileges.

The next day, the Assistant Director presented Joel with a bottle of Scotch.

"I suppose he wanted to make a good impression," Joel said.

Nor was this the end of life-style negotiations. The very next day he went to the prison hospital, having started to limp from a nail that stuck inside of a pair of prison-issued shoes. It was not an entirely necessary limp, Joel confessed to friends, but the Assistant Director had suggested that Joel might, in the near future, wish to visit the hospital, where "they have a very nice corner room and serve tea and crackers every day at mid-afternoon."

The nail in the shoe was, at the moment, the best he could come up with.

"You don't look too well," were the doctor's opening words.

Joel allowed as how he was feeling run down.

"What's wrong?" asked the doctor.

"I had hepatitis, once," Joel replied.

"Well, you'd better go to bed immediately."

It was a marvelous prescription and it was worth every bit of the 10,000 pesos it cost Joel. The hospital was not a Hilton Hotel, but by prison standards, it was about as good as could be attained. "We had nice private rooms, a kitchen, and a servant to take care of everything. We even had telephone service, in and out."

The alcohol situation was more than adequate, too, a bottle a day—rum, Japanese scotch, tequila. . . .

In another beneficial conversation with the doctor, it was decided that Joel should take a job in the hospital—neither his nail-in-shoe injury nor his earlier case of hepatitis being the best of medical reasons for a prolonged stay. Joel was first put in charge of the operating room, but was soon transferred to the storeroom which, as he admitted, was more logical for a man of his limited medical capacities.

Among his new duties, he kept inventory, including the supply of alcohol for medicinal purposes. Not too much of that treasure could be lifted, however, as "the administration stole half the supply before it even got there."

Joel also had a key to the pharmaceutical cabinet. "Now, that was worth a few experimental evenings when the liquor ran low."

One of the many benefits of hospital life was free access to the telephone. Joel could receive calls and, simply by picking up the infirmary phone and speaking to the operator, he could make outside calls. "Naturally, we charged all long-distance calls to the prison," he recalled.

"There were four of us in that section of the hospital, three Americans, all serving time for murder, and a Venezuelan named Carlos Antonio Contreras Castro, convicted of forging Mexican passports and travel documents for his comrades in the anti-Betancourt insurgency movement. Castro and I became quite close; he was a talkative but likable chap with an amazing talent for getting things done. While in jail, he conducted a brisk business obtaining passports for Spanish gypsies, using the phone to make arrangements through a contact in the Mexican government's Passport Division. He was able to secure Venezuelan documents through friends in the Consulate. Above all, he was exceptionally adept at getting whiskey into prison.

"By then, I had been drinking heavily, if intermittently, for several years and I'd been advised to stop for the damage it was doing to my body. I refused. If it was destroying my liver, it was lifting my spirits. One can go a bit mad in prison, even in the best of prison circumstances, and the wisdom that comes out of a bottle of Bacardi is sometimes extraordinarily protective of one's sanity.

"We would consume large quantities, and our wing (which came to be called 'The American Wing') began to smell more of rum than of antiseptics. Occasionally we would make our own brew, adding medicinal alcohol to the rum, throwing in some burnt sugar to give it taste and color, than a dash of hot chili to give it bite. It was called the Santa Marta Special, conceived by one of the Americans, a man named Brogan, who'd been around Mexican prisons since 1958. (Brogan had killed an Indian, which would probably not have done him in except he made the unforgivable mistake of stealing the governor's yacht as he fled the murder scene.)

"We became quite adept at improvising cocktails. If we had a supply of impure alcohol, we'd pour it into flat open pans and set a match to burn off the ether—then we'd mix it with grapefruit juice. A little raw, but not bad. And if we had some extra pure alcohol, well, that was beautiful stuff."

There is one night that stands out in Joel Kaplan's prison memories. Contreras Castro, Joel's talkative and venturesome roommate, was ill, an illness the doctor eventually diagnosed as venereal disease.

"Castro had developed this particularly irritating infection on the end of his penis. Unfortunately, it failed to respond to the ointments prescribed by the doctor. In fact, it appeared to grow worse. I told Castro that this problem would never have become so troublesome had he been circumcised. He kept jabbering away about that, damning his parents for not having saved him all this torment. He wouldn't shut up about it, and he was gradually driving the rest of us crazy.

"One Saturday night, after we had all consumed a particularly large quantity of rum, Castro was in particularly loud agony—staggering around the cell, wailing and whimpering, holding a half-empty fifth of Bacardi in one hand and his festering penis in the other. Finally one of us, I believe it was Brogan, suggested that we really ought to circumcise him there and then and be done with it.

"That stopped Castro as abruptly as if he'd run into a wall: 'You mean that?' he asked. Then he looked at me as though to ask, could it really be done? I shrugged, why not? He burst out laughing, like a man whose problems were about to be solved at last. 'Well, what are we waiting for?' he yelled.

"We went to the operating room, which was never locked, and turned on the surgical lights. There were three of us on the operating team—a young medical student; Brogan, who was a practical surgeon in the boy-scout emergency tradition; and myself.

"While we washed up and looked up the procedure in the medical books, Castro fortified himself with another bottle of Bacardi.

"The instruments were sterilized. Castro scampered up and down on the operating table, his pants dangling on the floor, and I gave him a shot, which knocked him out for a few minutes while the medical student gave him a local anesthetic. Apparently, he misjudged the amount of anesthetic that was needed, because Castro woke up in the middle of the operation and began screaming like a stuck pig.

"It was a bad moment. The medical student was holding down his arms; in one hand I was holding his penis by a pair of forceps and in the other hand the bottle of Bacardi from which the operating team was drinking; Brogan, knife in hand, was performing the surgery. Castro kept screaming, and I kept telling him to shut up, it would be over in a minute.

"Brogan went at it like a rabbi—and it was a neat job, if I say so. We fed Castro pain killers and Bacardi the rest of the night while we drank frequent toasts to our successful operation.

"Not only did we cure his infection, but the job was so well done that the next night Castro serviced a woman, or so he said."

"The old doctor who ran the hospital eventually fell sick from overindulging in booze. From what I could tell, the good doctor's wife assisted in his illness by nagging him to distraction. He died a week later, and from what we heard, she was largely responsible for that, too, managing to pull out the tubes that hung over his bed to nourish him.

"Then a new hospital head was assigned by the warden, and our reign of joy promptly ended. He was a man who didn't smoke, drink, or cohabit with women. It was obvious that one couldn't do a thing with a man like that. We all returned to the prison dormitory and the restrictions of a cell.

"It was really not too bad—though not nearly as free. The cell was about eight by ten. Double-decker cots. For a while, it was just Castro and myself and not crowded at all. I had a bed lamp, side table, bookcase for my steady supply of books, a cabinet for clothes. We had a hot plate to make our own coffee and tea and to heat up the dinners Irma would bring. The toilet was close by, just down the corridor from our cell. Cell doors were kept open except when we chose to lock them from the inside to protect against robberies; there are a lot of robberies in prison, you know. We had freedom to roam around the prison most of the day—mess, library, various shops, football field, dormitory courtyard. There were three roll calls a day to assure the guards of our presence: 6:10 A.M., 12:10, and 7:10 P.M. We were locked into our dormitory in the evenings, though we were free to move from cell to cell. Most prisoners did —chatting, playing cards, watching television in someone's cell. The guards were always around during the day and often in the evening. Our relationships with them were friendly enough, especially if you paid them off—a bit like bellhops at a hotel. They would do favors for you, minor things like delivering messages to the outside, making special calls, picking up needed items like books or anything not purchasable inside the walls. When it came to escapes, however, the guards were not valuable allies; there was simply too little they could do even if one assumed they would do it and not betray you. From what I could learn of them, they didn't have the guts to work on an escape.

"I never bothered much with other prisoners. Though I spent nine years in prisons—Coyoacan, Lecumberri, and Acatitla—I made no real friendships (except Contreras Castro) and preferred to stay mostly by myself. I spent much time reading. The prison library was reasonably well stocked with several thousand titles, many classics, an adequate supply of sociology and economics, political and historical studies; all in Spanish, of course. Irma and others would get me whatever other books I wanted.

"The food at Santa Marta wasn't too bad. Simple fare. Reasonable quality meat, chicken, beans, rice, stew. Mostly, however, I ate what Irma brought me. She's an excellent cook. Chops, fish, octopus, vegetables. She'd bring it in her large woolen purse, which was always full and included good whiskey. She enjoyed surprising me with various treats.

"They showed three movies a week at the prison theater, but I didn't go. I wasn't interested. My eyes could not focus properly and my hearing was not too good. Besides, the atmosphere in the theater was unpleasant. I suppose I was never a big fan of movies anyway.

"Santa Marta . . . 1967, 1968, 1969, 1970 . . . I became forty years old in prison.

"Birthdays have a way of making one extra sensitive to the passing of time. I had never been one who worried about growing old. I suppose I simply hadn't reached that age—until my fortieth birthday. It hit me very hard, much harder than I would have thought. To be sure, one becomes more conscious of age at periods of frustration and despair, one thinks how badly one's life is going and ponders the prospects for its improvement. I saw forty, and the prospects were frightening. I could not escape the even more frightening prospect that I might be turning fifty in that very same spot.

"I drank on that day. Irma brought me an excellent bottle of Scotch, beautifully wrapped it was, like a Christmas present. With a lovely smile, she took it out of that big woolen bag. She wanted me to have a party but she knew what was in my heart, and though she didn't want to show her awareness of what my anguish might be for fear of setting it off, I saw that she was crying when I drew away from our kiss. Inevitably, the day was dooming the both of us. We spent the next hour trying to conceal our feelings, both of us knowing that it was all a pretense.

"When she left, however, I could do nothing but attack that bottle of Scotch. I took it back to my cell with the eagerness of an alcoholic racing to a saloon.

"It was a very bad day."

During all those years in Lecumberri while his appeal had dragged on, Joel had lived with the thought he would eventually win a legal release. In fact, he'd been quite certain of it. He knew this was a classic response of prisoners the world over, but he still believed he would win out. Only with hindsight did he become aware of how naive and dense he had been, trusting the system of justice, believing the advice of counsel, and, in general, playing far too passive a role.

When the Mexican Supreme Court denied his appeal in September, 1967, irrevocably slamming the door, he had to face reality.

If he wanted to get out, he was going to have to escape.

Part Three

DEAD ENDS

15

For the next five years, Joel's thoughts were dominated by his drive to escape, gradually spiraling to near obsessive proportions. It became a source of agonizing frustration, but it was also the stuff of life—it was a stimulant to his creative energies, sharpening his mind, pressing him into action. It was an antidote to the classic affliction of long term prisoners: torpidity. The commitment alone was a statement of hope, and hope was the elixir that assuaged his pain.

For five years, escape plans would roll off his fecund brain like symphonies by Mozart. If they were not as brilliant, some of them were at least wildly imaginative. His mind proved to be highly adaptable to the ambience in which he lived, surprisingly so, for nothing in his life experience could have prepared him for what he had to face. But even in the rat-infested Lecumberri or the maximum security, murderer-dominated bastion of Acatitla, Joel managed to survive. More than that, he came to blend in with the way of life in a manner that far exceeded the expectations of those who knew him. In the spring of 1970, he even became a father. Irma gave birth to a daughter, Aura Guadalupe Isabel Kaplan, and Joel found an added inspiration to pursue his freedom.

107

If Joel learned from his earlier errors, it was his consummate agony that he would never learn enough to avoid making more. There were too many forces working against him, too many factors designed to defeat him. He would ride over many, only to find he needed one final thrust that he had not prepared for—and back he would go to the drawing board, a modern Sisyphus.

To his credit, he would always begin again.

"When it comes to breaking out of prison, I learned only one important thing: don't plan on it. A plan can be brilliant in thought and just as brilliant in execution, but pure old-fashioned luck will be the determining factor.

"An escape has to be a personal thing. Custom-made. Every situation is different, not only from prison to prison, but from section to section. The schedules vary. Every guard is different from every other. The slightest wrinkle in someone's personality will help you or destroy you. No man is so perceptive that he can figure out every little wrinkle, but he *can* know enough about his surroundings to give himself an edge.

"An escape plan has got to come out of you, out of your very specific situation. You've got to see it before you—like the proverbial light bulb going on in your head. It crosses your eyes during the routine course of the day, some facet of your prison life, some repeated exploitable occurrence, some new important bribable official.

"I stumbled onto such a possibility at Santa Marta in the prison hospital. One night, I was trying to sleep and not doing too well. A prisoner had been brought to the hospital that afternoon in pretty bad shape. At night, he became much worse, vomiting blood and running a high fever. I got up and did what I could to comfort him until the doctor came. A bleeding ulcer, the doc said, bad enough to call for surgery. Since, at that time, Santa Marta had neither operating equipment nor available personnel, the prisoner would have to be sent to the Mexico City General Hospital.

"I watched them lay him on a stretcher and wheel him out, and from the hospital window, I saw them pack him into an ambulance.

"It was early morning when I got back to my own bed, but there was no way I could get back to sleep— not with an image of a large ambulance driving through that front gate.

"The light bulb was flashing in my head.

"The gate, yes. A big chain-link metal structure. It stands forbiddingly just outside the administration building of the prison, guarded by two men with rifles and side arms, overlooked by two sentries with rifles in the towers that are on top of the prison wall beside the gate. One cannot sneak under it, over it, or around it. One can only pass through it.

"In an ambulance, say."

Joel began to set up a plan. Simple enough; he would fake a terrible pain from acute appendicitis. Surely, one could fool these doctors with a phony attack. He went to the prison library and read up on that useless organ.

Joel then approached the prison ambulance driver. There appeared to be no doubt of his willingness to help. It was purely a matter of money. He asked for 75,000 pesos (about $5200) and Joel agreed. Then he asked for one-third in advance, even before other details had been worked out: he needed to make repairs on the ambulance, he said, adding that, since he would have to go out of his assigned route for the getaway, he wanted to spread a few thousand pesos around to cover it, just to protect himself. Again, Joel agreed.

He scraped up some more cash. It was no easy thing for Joel Kaplan, the millionaire, to get his hands on his own money. He had to ask his uncle for everything; and his uncle parceled out money as if with an eye-dropper.

J. M. Kaplan sent Joel an allowance that was "money enough to keep me in razor blades, magazines, alcohol, and women, but no money for me to buy my way out of prison," Joel recalls, bitterly.

The differences in perspectives between a jail cell in Mexico City and an office building in New York City can be more than the miles involved. While Joel felt hamstrung by his uncle's apparent parsimony with his inheritance, J. M. Kaplan obviously felt he was protecting Joel's best interests by not letting him squander his funds on bribes that wouldn't work. And so the financier indicated in one of his letters to Joel:

> Meanwhile, have it clear in your mind that the money you now receive steadily is much *more than ample* [emphasis in original] to cover the reasonable requirements of Irma Vasquez and all the others who provide you with petty services and minor requirements. Also bear in mind, Joel, that giving money to bloodsuckers can only strengthen the chains that imprison you. . . . For yourself, personally, you can have anything I am saving for you; in fact, anything I am able to give or do. . . .

Then why, Joel repeatedly asked himself, in an anguished and often feverish interior monologue, *why couldn't he, Joel Kaplan, be allowed to spend some of his own money to try to save his own life?*

Through the good offices of Irma, who smuggled letters past the guards to mail to his sister Judy, Joel had arranged for an "outside man"—an adventurous Canadian friend of Judy's named Dempsey—to aid in his getaway.

He would meet the ambulance as it was driven to an intersection three miles from Santa Marta, lead it into an unpopulated side road and presume to kidnap Joel at gunpoint, thereby protecting the ambulance driver from being charged with complicity. Joel would immediately change clothes while being driven to a second car—the old hot car to cold car technique—in which two women would be waiting, one posing as the Canadian's wife, the other as Joel's, and the four would then drive innocently northward, a group of happy tourists on the way back to the States.

Joel waited for the ambulance driver to give the go-ahead, but when he saw him again, he was told there were problems. When Joel asked what such problems might be, the driver replied that he couldn't talk about it any more and hurried away. The explanation for this strange conduct reached Joel on the following afternoon when he was in his room at the hospital, reading on his bed; a hospital attendant came in with his pail and mop and began swabbing the floor.

"Señor Kaplan . . . I need some money."

Joel looked up, nonplussed.

"I need 5000 pesos," the man continued.

"For what?" Joel finally asked.

"You will pay me because I have to help you get away in the ambulance."

Joel knew that the driver had put him up to it, his way of blackmailing Joel into still another payment. Joel controlled his temper and his impatience, especially since his dependence on the driver was nothing short of total. Of course, the driver knew that and offered no apologies. In fact, he even had the gall to ask for more money himself, to which Joel replied that he'd get more, a lot more, as soon as he drove him out, but not until then.

And so that, too, was agreed upon. But three days later, the hospital attendant was mopping the floor again, and though he had as yet been paid nothing, the man appeared to be terribly amused. Joel himself heard the news later that night.

The ambulance driver, celebrating his anticipated newfound fortune in advance, had gone on a boisterous drinking spree and had been fired for reporting to work drunk.

16

One of Joel's visitors at Acatitla was his brother Ezra. A quiet, subdued man, younger than Joel by three years and taller by half a foot, he worked as a computer analyst at Columbia University, living alone in a modest apartment near the campus on New York's Upper West Side.

They chatted, these two laconic brothers, friendly enough yet not knowing each other. To Joel, Ezra was an extremely conservative man who already seemed considerably older than he was. To Ezra, Joel seemed on the brink of total disaster brought on by the profligacy he appeared to have chosen for himself years before. If they had never been close in the past, they were far more distant now.

Despite the differences in their life styles, Ezra was not without compassion for his brother's plight and wanted to do whatever he could to help.

But how?

After so many years in stir, Joel could rattle off a fresh variation on the theme at the mere mention of the word "escape." What Ezra had no way of knowing was with what degree of seriousness he should react to anything Joel told him. Now, Joel was proposing a new ploy, which Ezra was to take back to New York with him, a rather bizarre idea that required $100,000 to bribe several medics and health officials who would declare Joel dead. Joel would then be taken out in a black bag and delivered to a carefully chosen—and bribed—funeral home. There, his body would be switched with a dead one, and while that body was being buried, Joel would be on his way to Peru.

Well, why not, Ezra thought. If it had been good enough for Luis Vidal, Jr., it should be good enough for Joel. Wouldn't it make perfect sense for Joel to think he might be able to escape by the same ruse he said had been used to bring off his conviction?

Ezra returned to New York. A week later, he wrote Joel that he had asked Uncle Jack, the trustee of their inheritances, for the $100,000.

Uncle Jack said no.

Said Joel, later: "The way my luck was running anyway, the substitute corpse was likely to rat on me."

Another family visitor was Joel's Uncle Henry, "The Colonel," as he was called. "The Colonel," said Joel, "received his commission during World War II through contacts made at the bar of the Waldorf Astoria Hotel, where he maintained a suite. He was a real charmer, a born whiskey salesman, and he knew how to spread his favors where they did the most good. His suite at the Waldorf was available to influential friends—and so was his little black book with telephone numbers of available girls. If the war had lasted a few more years, Henry would have made general." After the war, Henry Kaplan went back to Schenley, a company he had worked for since Repeal. In the late 1940's, he left Schenley and opened Quality Importers, handling such brands as Hiram Walker, Ambassador Scotch, and Bushmills.

He was taller than his brothers, a distinguished-looking man with a full head of silvery hair. He dressed

113

stylishly, wore a flashy diamond ring, and was the only one of the Kaplan brothers with a true flair for sociability. Henry Kaplan liked people and people liked him. Especially important people. Even important people like Meyer Lansky. According to Susan Rosenstiel, once married to Schenley liquor tycoon Lewis Rosenstiel, it was an old relationship: "I, myself, saw Lansky together with both Henry and Jack Kaplan at the Fountainbleu Hotel in Miami Beach in 1957, when Lansky flew up from Havana to see them." Mrs. Rosenstiel adds that Henry's suite at the Waldorf was always available to his friends at the hotel: "Lucky Luciano (alias Charley Ross), Bugsy Siegel (who lived there with actress Wendy Barrie), and even Frank Costello. Henry would actually oblige them all by turning his room into a sort of casino."

He was a sporting man, a big race-track enthusiast who had a reputation for placing bets that ran into five figures. He always made money, and he enjoyed spending it.

Not the least of his activities was related to his brother Jack's affairs. Henry and Jack maintained close business associations long after the bootlegging years. Though Jack became powerful in highly respectable circles in government, the arts, education, and philanthropy, Henry's associations did not appear to distress him. Indeed, Jack did not hesitate to involve his younger brother whenever he felt Henry could be of service.

As with this trip to Mexico City in 1968, Henry came to Santa Marta Acatitla Prison bearing a case of Jack Daniels—to be delivered through Irma's devices, bottle by bottle. A considerate gift—or so Joel thought until Irma subsequently received a bill for the whiskey. Said Joel: "All Henry gave me was a Quality Importers' promotional pen and a copy of *Playboy*."

Uncle Henry also brought tidings of hope from Jack: if their friend Hubert Humphrey defeated Nixon in the coming election, the new President could be counted on to intercede personally in securing Joel's release. According to Joel, Henry also told him that "if Nixon were elected, he and Jack had a line of approach through John Mitchell, whose law firm had represented the Kaplans at one time or another. So I drank the excellent whiskey and was foolish enough to believe him."

But the real purpose of the Colonel's visit was something else again. Bonnie, whom Joel had never divorced, had been kicking up a considerable fuss, placing long-distance phone calls loaded with protestations of love and demands for money. In Uncle Henry's opinion, the solution to the problem was divorce, which would obviously mean a substantial financial settlement. All Joel had to do was sign over power of attorney to Henry. With this in hand, he could proceed.

Joel took a celebratory swig of Jack Daniels and reached for a pen. Henceforth, all his problems would be handled by Uncle Henry.

Or so Joel believed.

Henry Kaplan had also visited Joel's sister Judy in San Francisco to obtain power of attorney from her. He told her that her father's affairs were finally being cleared up, that they were really too complicated to explain, and that there was a question of federal taxes only he and Uncle Jack, with all their influence, could bring to an advantageous settlement with the government. "He said he was going to save me $200,000," Judy remembers.

But Judy balked. She told Henry she thought she ought to talk to an attorney.

Henry asked Judy to meet with him to discuss the matter. On his instructions, she went to an office in the liquor warehouse of Max Sobel, a large San Francisco distributor with whom he did business. There, she recalls, he "read me the riot act. He told me I needed his and Uncle Jack's skilled hands to administer my funds, that both of them had always acted in my best interests, that my refusal to sign made me seem ungrateful for all they'd done in the past. I finally said, 'Oh hell, all right,' and signed the paper."

What neither Joel nor Judy then knew was that they had signed legal control of their multimillion-dollar inheritance over to J. M. Kaplan. Lovable Uncle Henry had acquired their two essential signatures for hated Uncle Jack.

The Kaplan children's complicated financial history began in 1936 when their father, A. I. Kaplan, decided that $7.5 million of his estate should be put in trust for his three children. At the heart of the trust was Nemtico—New Mexico Timber Company—which A. I. had founded and nurtured into an enormous financial success. In 1958–59, at the time he was dying, A. I. bequeathed Nemtico outright to his now-grown heirs. But at this point, after decades of estrangement, Jack approached his brother and effected a dialogue if not a full reconciliation. A. I. became convinced that Joel, Ezra, and Judy were incapable of handling such a large sum of money, and on his deathbed, he appointed his brother Jack as executor of his estate.

Both Joel and Judy say their father's executor never informed them of the original Nemtico bequest.

Under the terms of their father's bequest, Nemtico —which was by then a holding company for the millions that had come from the sale of New Mexico timberlands—was to be dissolved after ten years. At that point, the proceeds were to be equally distributed among the three heirs.

In 1968, when Uncle Henry made his visits to Joel and Judy, the ten-year deadline was approaching. Had their signatures not been obtained, the Nemtico millions would have had to be handed outright to the heirs by J. M. Kaplan who, as executor, had control of the funds.

Using the powers of attorney obtained in that

el David Kaplan at about the age of
fteen, when he was a student at the
ew Mexico Military Institute.

the late 1950's, the marital hassles
Joel and Bonnie were almost a
gular feature of the *Daily News*.
his story appeared in the edition of
ne 25, 1958.

Sugar Close to Molasses?

Will blonde
model Bonnie
Shari, 23, go
back to her
wealthy mo-
lasses dealer
husband, Joel
D. Kaplan, 31?
Or will she press
the separation
suit she brought
last January,
along with a re-
quest for $2,000
a month tempo-
rary alimony
and $35,000 in
counsel fees?
Yesterday the
couple and their
lawyers went
into a huddle in
the chambers of
Supreme Court
Julius Cans on
a possible rec-
onciliation.. He
gave them until
tomorrow to
make up their
minds. We'll let
you know.

(NEWS foto by Al Pucci)
The Joel D. Kaplans yesterday.

Luis Vidal, Jr.—sometime business
partner and alleged victim of Joel
Kaplan.

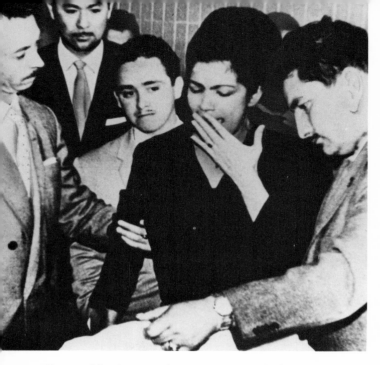

Above: Mexican authorities accepted this woman's statement that she was the wife of Luis Vidal, Jr. She is shown here, in Mexico, identifying the body.
Below left: Joel David Kaplan in 1958: The respectable businessman.
Below right: Joel David Kaplan in 1963: The convicted murderer.

Above: A. I. Kaplan, Joel's father.
Right: Ray Kaplan, Joel's mother.

"Uncle Jack"—J. M.
Kaplan in 1967.

Opposite, top: The prison yard at Santa Marta Acatitla.

Opposite, bottom: August 19, 1971: Detectives search the cell Joel Kaplan and Carlos Contreras Castro so lately fled.

Left: Back home in Glendora, Vic Stadter talks about the escape.

Below: The copter captured. Mexican police stand guard over the escape vehicle.

Better days in Guadalajara. Car
Contreras Castro prior to his stay
Santa Marta Acatitla Prison.

Better days are here again. Carl
Contreras Castro holds a press co
ference in Caracas after the escap
With him is his lawyer, Dr. Nan
Campos de Morales.

...e of three Polaroid shots used to ...sure Joel Kaplan's attorneys that he ...s alive and well in California.

...low, left to right: ...union in California: Joel and his ...ter, Judy Dowis; with Vic Stadter; ...th his attorney, Vasilios Choulos; ...d with Irma.

Joel and Irma celebrating in the United States.

eleventh hour, J. M. Kaplan dissolved Nemtico. Ezra, who had been quick to go along with his uncle's wishes, received his share outright. But the millions owed Joel and his sister Judy were locked up in a new trust in which both heirs were denied control of their own money. They were to receive subsistence money from the interest on their capital, but were not allowed to touch the principal without the approval, in writing, of their uncles.

Joel was stunned when he later discovered what he had done on signing that piece of paper: "I'd been had. I had agreed to turn over control of my money to my Uncle Jack—and at the very time I needed it most. Feeling the way I do about my uncle, why would I ever have knowingly permitted him such control over my fate?"

His rancor was well founded, especially given one particular clause in the new trust, a clause that stated Joel could have access to the principal only if he were "freely established in a state of the United States of America."

One does not have to be an expert in trusts to read this wrinkle as something of a double whammy against Joel. At the time he signed over power of attorney— and, effectively, his money—Joel had some twenty years yet to serve in Mexico on his murder sentence. In the normal course of events, that would make him unavailable to request his inheritance in the United States until he was sixty-two. If Joel was to get his money at any time substantially before he was ready to collect social security, he would have to be pardoned or exonerated by the Mexican government. Everyone connected with Joel's bizarre imprisonment and trial agreed such a miracle was clearly not in the offing.

And even if Joel did manage to escape from prison —despite his uncle's refusal to provide any money for the pursuit of that possibility—he faced another and even knottier problem: How could a convicted mur-

117

derer and jailbreaker from a Mexican penitentiary possibly enter the United States so as to reside there, as the language in the trust made necessary, "openly and freely."

"The way he wrote up my trust, I couldn't get that money unless I was settled in a little rose-covered cottage in suburbia. What if I escaped to another country? What if I couldn't get back into the United States? What if I didn't want to return?"

Those were indeed tough questions, and Joel had no answers. To get by this particular crown of thorns seemed a job for a superman—and one who would work on credit, at that.

17

To Judy Kaplan Dowis, the thought of her brother being stuck in a Mexican jail was, as she put it, "a mind-blower." She simply could not understand—or tolerate—his being there. She was not the kind of cerebral person adept at analyzing problems in depth. She could not recount the intricacies of the law involved in his incarceration. She didn't care about the judicial process. She was a person who *felt* the injustice and reacted with an uncompromising intensity. If the judicial process had put him there, then some other way had to be found to get him out. She didn't care how, or by whom, or for how much.

Judy was a strange lady. She had always been so. She remembered childhood as a series of frightening images that sent her clinging to mother in awe of father. Her adolescence was, like Joel's, emotionally unrewarding and left her bewildered by life. At nineteen, she had no idea as to who she was or what she wanted. The thing she was least prepared for was marriage—so she got married, hoping to free herself from her background. It was a mistake. Her husband was in the fabrics business. She went to work in his office as a receptionist expected to charm his buyers, but ended up rebelling against that aggressive and frenetic world.

A competitor in New York's tough garment district

proved no soul mate to a young girl struggling for identity, and inevitably, the marriage folded. Judy went on to find gratification in the different values of Greenwich Village painters and eventually, she married again, this time a painter-sculptor named David Dowis. She bore him three children in a marriage that was wild, unpredictable, and eventually trouble-filled. When it ended, they split for different parts of the world.

She was now a woman in her thirties with a tremendous capacity for growth. She had her children and enough money for her needs and pleasures. She was artistic, spiritual, and extremely sensitive. She found her children to be beautiful, having learned what it was to be responsible and to care for someone in the deepest sense of the word—an experience alien to her own childhood surroundings.

Judy describes herself as coming from "a long line of profiteers, of ice-cold business squares with their hate showing, of brothers and cousins clawing each other like jackals for the carcass and nobody ever caring about others. I remember the story my mother told me—about an entry she found in my father's diary after he died. When my father had gone broke, he went to his brother for help, and my mother said Uncle Jack made him get down on his knees and crawl across the floor to him. . . . Jesus! And these are the type of people who think hippies are nuts!"

Like Joel's, her childhood had been emotionally deprived. Their father, a tough Spartan moody man would defy nature by walking bare-chested on winter mornings across their farm in South Salem, New York. He was a brilliant self-educated man, an amateur expert in geopolitics, a builder who loved to do things himself, even to chopping his own firewood. His wife, Ray, was a quiet, competent Brooklyn-born woman of German descent, who tended to the house and children and was busy with the social life of the area. All very proper but, as it turned out, stultifying in its impact on the children.

"We were these three crazy Kaplan kids, all from the same two parents, growing up in the same places and all. But you couldn't find three people anywhere who are so completely unalike and so obviously nuts. Like with money, for example: Ezra counts every penny of it and never spends any. Joel squanders it, loves it, works for it. And me, I don't even know what it looks like," Judy has said.

Judy was the artist, the esthete, the tranquility-seeker. When her mood ran to melancholy, she would go off to Santa Fe and the peace of the desert, painting pictures of sand and sky and distant hills, letting her mind float to some other plateau where reality could not intrude.

Realities frightened her. Like her brother being in jail. She could not cope with that. She only knew that somehow he had to get out of that horrible place.

She had watched her mother slowly kill herself working to free Joel—hiring lawyers, bribing officials, waiting countless hours in the anterooms of men of influence on both sides of the Mexican border, spending hundreds of thousands of dollars. For nothing. Her grief at her mother's death was hardened by the knowledge that Ray had worn herself down in vain. There was no legal way to get her brother out of jail.

There was one other fact Judy had to accept: she was now the only one left in her family who would do anything, legal or illegal, to free Joel.

To begin that most difficult task, she picked the toughest turf in America: the paramilitary shadowland of Miami. In the 1960's, Miami was a city of spies and counterspies, of unemployed soldiers of fortune, of fanatics for causes and killers for hire. It was a city of a half-million uprooted Cubans, of big-time gunrunning and major-league dope dealing, of FBI agents spying on CIA agents, of bitter commando groups stubbornly training in the swamps and keys of southern Florida for invasions that would never be launched. It was no place for a lady on her own. Luck, in a perverse, roundabout, and costly sort of way, was to be with the lady.

It began with a beach party at which Judy was introduced to tow-haired, handsome Martin Francis Xavier Casey, a half-Irish, half-Cuban American in his late twenties. Casey was the self-styled "archivist" of all the anti-Castro groups operating in the Miami area. He knew everyone and everything and was in on plenty, though his boy-next-door looks and his parochial school politeness belied his activist credentials.

Through Casey, Judy gained entrée to a tight-knit circle of paramilitary Don Quixotes with headquarters in a rambling tan clapboard rooming house on Southwest Fourth Street in an old section of Miami not far from the Cuban *barrio.* The boarding house was run by Nelli Hamilton, a motherly lady who asked few questions and whose strictest rule of conduct was that no guns be brought to the dinner table. Nelli wasn't bothered when a roomer walked through her living room cheerfully swinging a Coca-Cola six-pack filled with grenades, but she yelled like hell if he hadn't wiped his feet before coming in.

Her boarders were a strange assortment of ex-Green Berets, occasional CIA contract pilots and military "advisers," acrobatic ex-convicts, and guns-for-hire. All of them wanted to do good—for a price. And all continued to smoke the long pipe of overthrowing Castro, or any other government near enough and small enough to do in. After a few beers, they would laughingly refer to themselves as "The Soldiers of Misfortune," a jibe at their propensity for picking losing sides.

Their record did not deter Judy from asking their help. Nor did it deter them from trying, especially when the attractive lady who liked to wear Hopi Indian blankets showed that she could back up her request with cash.

For several years, Judy's life would be divided between caring for her children in her ranch-style Coconut Grove home and being both key contractor and den mother to the inhabitants of Nelli Hamilton's boarding house. One by one, they came to her with schemes to free Joel. She tried a good many of the schemes, even the most preposterous. The problem itself was so crazy, she could hardly avoid considering crazy solutions.

In this wild setting, Judy financed various escape plots, conceived and hatched and put into operation by the Soldiers of Misfortune. All were similarly futile. One such scheme, implemented by a tall, rawboned, sandy-haired ex-CIA operative named Jack Carter, was typical. Carter had done contract work for the CIA flying air strikes against oil tanks near Havana. His plan to liberate Joel was right in keeping with his background. For openers, he "borrowed" Judy's Jaguar, then drove to Mexico City with a multifaceted game plan involving a fire in the prison linen-storage room; a phony linen supply truck driven by two Cuban exiles, who would drive Joel out; and a professional mountaineer from the Tyrolean Alps (known as "The Hiker") who would lead Joel on an arduous trek to a plane hidden in the distant hills. Later, when Joel learned of it all, his only comment was "That's the work of an idiot!"

Judy says, "That bastard Carter still owes me a Jaguar." But Carter says he used all the money he got from the sale of the car on the escape.

The Jaguar, however, was a small matter when stacked up against the mountains of cash Judy was dispensing, mostly in small bills. She would find herself repeatedly going to the bank, cashing huge checks to finance one scheme or another, "until money seemed like crumbs to a flock of pigeons. I mean, that bank teller would look at me, 'You're crazy,' his eyes would say, and then he'd try his mouth: 'Mrs. Dowis, you shouldn't be taking out all this cash, not so carelessly anyway. It isn't safe.' I mean, I'd have to argue to get my own money, then he'd look at me with his mouth open as I'd stuff the thirty grand in an old envelope without even counting it."

Judy's expenditures on futile escape plots came to a considerable sum. Still, she found ways to extract the money from the Wall Street lawyers handling her trust fund without giving them an inkling of what she was about: $20,000 for "a real estate transaction"; $12,500 for "home improvements"; $15,000 for "educational allowances for my three children"; $4,000 for "a second car." And so it went. It would be over three years before Judy would find the man who could get Joel out, and before then she would spend substantially over $200,-000 in this piecemeal manner.

One of the Soldiers of Misfortune befriended by Judy was Jerry Porter. Balding, nearing fifty, but blue-eyed and debonair, Porter was a World War II PT-boat commander and naval hero, a former male model and occasional pillhead who has said he was in charge of CIA arms shipments out of New Orleans preparatory to the Bay of Pigs. ("I didn't want the job but the CIA had enough on me to void my passport if I didn't co-operate.")

Jerry Porter didn't come to Judy for money. He came looking for a place to hide from gun-toting creditors. All she knew was that Porter's latest scheme—an exploration submarine with a huge glass window in which he had planned to take the guests of a leading Miami Beach hotel for rides under Biscayne Bay—had blown up in his face when his drunken partner had loudly told the hotel manager, who was even then about to sign the contract, that all his guests would see on the bottom of the Bay were "the feces of millionaires and the bodies of mob victims."

Judy let Commander Porter hide out in her house.

As later events would show, her befriending of Porter was to be the pivotal factor in turning Joel's luck.

The unusual relationship that developed between Judy and these adventurers paid other, unexpected dividends. Rough, dangerous men, their talents and loyalties for hire, they responded to Judy's innocent befriending with an unexpected honesty. Judy particularly remembers the one-armed Canadian named Dempsey, a boarding house regular who had been sent to Mexico to help get Joel out of the country once he'd broken prison in the ambulance escape. When the ambulance driver got drunk and the escape aborted, Dempsey returned to Miami. With him he brought $6,000 in cash— unused expense and bribe money Judy had given him. One morning soon after his return, Dempsey rang Judy's doorbell and handed over the money. "He could as easily have kept it and fed me some story about having paid it all out in Mexico," Judy says.

Judy finally gave up on Miami and moved to Sausalito. "I knew so little geography I thought San Francisco was closer to Mexico City anyway."

The change in locale did not alter her lifestyle, but she did encounter a set of political attitudes very different from those held by the Miami ex-CIA, anti-Castro types. The adventurers and putative escape artists Judy came on in the Bay Area were of a more New Left bent. Many were roustabouts and ne'er-do-wells and, collectively, they were known as Sausalito wharf rats.

Judy's home in Sausalito was "beautiful, wild, crazy." Located high on a winding, frequently fog-bound hillside road named Cloud View, it hung over the San Francisco Bay like an old-fashioned castle, a Moorish-Spanish mansion with turrets and hanging gardens.

The word soon spread along the waterfront that the rich lady in the big house was looking for someone to break her brother out of a Mexican jail. Judy's home became a stopping-off point and watering hole for every stray from Big Sur to Mendecino. Most of these wharf rats had engaged at various times in relatively light illegal activities—smuggling grass or poaching abalone. But for money, they were prepared to try something heavier—or at least to talk about it. Unfortunately for Judy, these West Coast adventurers displayed none of the old-fashioned chivalry of the Miami contingent. They moved in on her as though she were running some sort of public hostelry, and they fed off her generosity with no consideration for her needs. For a time, she was helpless, overwhelmed by their numbers and incessant demands. She would retreat into corners of her home with her children, spending all her time with them, sick at what she had allowed to happen, this exploitation of her compassion. Her brother was rotting in jail while these rip-off artists were draining her dry.

One day, it all became too much for her, and she sat down at her typewriter and wrote five words on a single sheet of paper:

"This is MY house, dammit!"

The wharf rats of Sausalito were scattered by the arrival of a new figure in Judy's life. A venturesome Westerner with New Left politics, he was called, simply, "Lewis." Lewis was one of Big Sur's nomadic citizens, but he was also the leader of an amorphous organization known as the Big Sur Rangers—a home-made peace-keeping group in that wild territory of strays.

Lewis, who had close ties with leading rock musicians and often acted as business agent for these friends, looked a man of mystery: Dressed in black jeans and a black silk shirt, he always had a long knife obvious and ever ready in his belt. Yet one of his good friends was Vasilios Choulos, a partner in Melvin Belli's

law firm. Choulos often handled the rock businessman's legal affairs.

Judy and Lewis connected through Judy's sister-in-
law, Ginny Dowis. Ginny had bought Lewis's house in
Big Sur and, during the small talk between buyer and
seller, she had mentioned Judy's Olympian efforts to
get Joel out of a Mexican jail. When Lewis said it might
just be a job for the Big Sur Rangers, Ginny picked up
the phone.

One result of that telephone call was the beginning
of the significant Belli-Kaplan liaison. After listening to
Judy's story, Lewis said it sounded as if she and Joel
needed some heavy legal help and he suggested Belli's
firm had the kind of non-Establishment reputation that
might turn the trick. One week later, an eye-catching
trio boarded a plane bound for Mexico City: the sartor-
ially elegant Melvin Belli, his long white mane blowing
in the wind; the modishly attired and mustachioed
Vasilios Choulos; and Judy, a brown Hopi Indian blanket wrapped around her shoulders.

In Mexico City, Belli renewed a long acquaintance
with Victor Velasquez, who briefed the San Francisco
lawyers on the strange and frustrating legal history of
Joel Kaplan. The trio then visited Joel in prison, a visit
that resulted in the Belli firm more or less becoming
general counsel to the Kaplan brother and sister. Thus
began a long period of sorting out the tangled legal
and financial knots that tied their respective fortunes.

Back home in Sausalito, Judy called Lewis. Her
brother, she told him, had whispered to her that he had
set up his escape and that he needed a trustworthy person in Mexico City to handle the arrangements. Would
Lewis go?

He promised to be on the next plane out.

A day later, the head of the Big Sur Rangers was
shaking hands with Joel Kaplan in Santa Marta Acatitla prison.

Joel, it seemed, had been dangling a fat carrot in

front of the warden's nose. Not without success, it appeared. He felt that the warden and he had won each other's confidence and that a bribe would be very much in order. For a sum in the neighborhood of $30,000, the warden was making noises to suggest that he would drive Joel through the prison gate and deliver him to friends.

Obviously, the first step was to deliver a substantial portion of this sum up front. Lewis advised against it, arguing that such payment made it too simple for the warden to back out. Joel kept insisting that the warden would make no move without it. For openers, then, Lewis was to go back to Judy and secure the money— which Lewis adamantly refused to do, telling Joel it would be a waste.

Joel, however, was not without resources. Like a great trial lawyer who needs to pull a dramatic coup in front of a hostile jury, Joel marched Lewis directly into the warden's office, barging in like a man of power and prestige. He picked up the warden's phone in his presence and called San Francisco.

"I need $10,000 in cash" he demanded of Choulos, who was now handling Joel's "allowance" from his trust fund. "I want you to give it to Lewis."

Lewis was stunned, and tremendously impressed. He would do what was asked of him. On his return to San Francisco, he sent the money to Irma who, in turn, delivered it to the warden, and the preparations for the driveout began. Lewis, meanwhile, began to arrange for the getaway. He made a deal with Judy to be paid expenses plus a small percentage cut of whatever Joel might gain from the realization of his father's estate.

Joel's deal with the warden was to get him outside the prison; it was Lewis's job to get him out of Mexico and safely into the United States. It was an assignment Lewis approached with some trepidation, fearing that, even if the warden delivered on his contract, he might just cover himself once outside the prison by shooting

128

Joel and claiming the credit for stopping an escape. Lewis visited San Diego, where the Big Sur Rangers' expert in armaments was resident. It was decided that the safest vehicle to drive Joel Kaplan out of Mexico would be an armored car. A Brinks item would be indiscreet, so the Rangers proceeded to forge a modified version. Lewis purchased a 1969 Pontiac, installed bulletproof glass, and stuffed flack jackets in the door panels and behind the rear seat. Lewis also arranged with a retired Air Force colonel in San Diego to fly into Mexico and pick up Joel when the makeshift armored car had reached a spot safe enough for a plane to land. He tapped two Rangers for duty in Mexico; one drove the escape car across the border, and the other flew to Mexico City with Lewis, who had scheduled a final meeting with Joel.

Before they left, the Rangers acquired weapons suitable for most contingencies—a hot .38 caliber revolver stolen from the California Highway Patrol along with special armor-piercing bullets, two Israeli Ouzi submachine guns, and assorted smaller side arms. They also carried a sack full of cash for expenses and such additional bribes as might prove necessary.

Joel told Lewis that the warden hadn't yet given him a firm date. It was agreed that the two Rangers would remain in Mexico City with the armored escape car. Lewis would return to San Francisco and wait for a signal from Joel, who said he would telephone when the warden gave him the three-day countdown signal. "I could just picture Joel walking into that warden's office and placing the call to me, saying it was three days to zero or something like that," Lewis says. "It was unreal."

The unreal remained unrealized as weeks dragged into months. The Rangers remained stationed in Mexico City, the obliging Air Force colonel remained on the alert in San Diego, and Lewis stayed near his phone. Irma called several times to say that things appeared ready, but then would call back the next day to say it had been a false alarm. After four months, and some $12,000 invested in expenses and equipment, Lewis visited Joel for a small summit meeting. Joel reluctantly agreed that the warden's eyes for money were bigger than his stomach to carry out the escape; he was bribable, all right, but too frightened to go beyond accepting a down payment. Lewis signaled the Rangers to retreat back to Big Sur. He himself went to Hawaii—"for a vacation."

According to Judy, it was just as well that nothing had moved according to Joel's plan: Lewis had told her he'd "got into" Tarot cards during his long vigil by the phone, and had read nothing but death messages in them.

18 In mid-October of 1970, a young Mexican named Alonzo Corales and his wife bought title to a rather desolate tract of land on a dry lake bed a few miles outside the village of Santa Marta. In early November, a two-and-a-half ton truck delivered a large quantity of prefabricated building material to the site. A few days later, the same truck brought a group of Corales's friends who had come to help. Had anyone asked what Corales was doing on such a barren spot, he would have been told that Corales was a chicken farmer about to build a business on the site with the help of his friends. Indeed, within a week, there was a large chicken shed with over a hundred baby chicks pecking at the feed generously spread around the area.

The Coraleses, meanwhile, established residence in a large but flimsy trailer parked on the premises. There they were joined each day by their friends. Anyone near enough to notice would have seen Señor Corales and his friends enter the chicken shed each morning, coming out only for the meals that Señora Corales prepared in the trailer.

In fact, the only eyes within range belonged to the guards stationed in the tower abutting the courtyard of Dormitory Number Two of the Acatitla Prison. What these guards were unable to see inside the chicken shed, some 200 yards away, was not an increasing brood of chickens but a rising mound of earth. Its significance was its destination: a tunnel was in construction aimed directly at the courtyard of Dormitory Number One.

It was in this courtyard that the prisoner Joel David Kaplan took his daily walks.

Joel had heard of all those great tunnel escapes during World War II. The trouble with duplicating this scheme at Santa Marta was the impracticality of digging through concrete floors. One needed pneumatic drills, pick axes, shovels, wheelbarrows, dozens of willing workers, and the dumbest collection of guards that the world of penology might ever know. Where, for example might all that dirt be concealed? One could picture the toilet and sewage systems being clogged with it.

For a single man, or even a dozen operating in total secrecy for a year, it was a totally impractical plan. One could simply not dig his way out of Acatitla.

But to dig a tunnel in?

Irma knew an engineer and proceeded to ask him about its possibilities, baiting him with earnest money. After examining the area around the prison, he agreed that it was an unlikely dig, but possible. The question was, how much water lay how deep beneath the surface? How penetrable was the lava rock? Though he admitted a two-hundred-yard tunnel was a difficult and risky venture, he agreed to give it a try. He predicted that six men working in shifts could dig out as much as thirty feet a day. Four weeks work, then, should complete the job.

Joel began counting off feet on his calendar. Indeed, the thought of those men burrowing under the ground, unseen by anyone, coming closer and closer to his courtyard, was more gratifying than any escape idea he'd yet conjured. He would walk by the towering wall under which they would be digging and feel a delicious tingling under the collar. He began to wonder at the degree of accuracy with which the tunnel could be brought to a specific area of the courtyard. For example, there was a corner behind the basketball court that was frequently used to collect garbage: at the appropriate time, Joel could amass a convenient pile to conceal his exit.

There were other problems, such as timing the escape. What time would be the most propitious? Presumably during a meal when the courtyard was less likely to be populated. Of the three dining periods, the most suitable would be lunch when the sun was hot; even those who chose not to eat would not be out baking themselves. And if there chanced to be anyone around, Joel could poke about in the garbage pretending he had lost something until he felt the moment was right to disappear.

The problem was to have the engineer reach the surface and open the hole at a prearranged time, perhaps at a signal, then collapse the entrance immediately after Joel climbed in. He considered taking a few others with him, but hesitated to let anyone in on the plan until the final moment for fear of word getting out.

At the end of the sixth day of tunneling, however, Irma came with the news: the chicken farmers had hit a thick vein of lava rock. The engineer had tested adjacent areas but there was no way to continue around the lava.

Irma said the engineer had cried when he told her.

But Irma was laughing.

Joel had never seen Irma laugh at the collapse of one of his escape plans. She didn't explain, but simply reached into her huge wool bag and pulled out the chicken dinner she had cooked for his supper that day.

19

In the spring of 1970, Judy Kaplan Dowis began hearing disquieting reports about the physical and mental condition of her brother. Those who had visited Joel came away with a strong sense of his impending death. His pallor was exceptional. He trembled as he spoke. His body appeared to be so frail that any further attacks of hepatitis would likely kill him. Alcohol was both a symptom and an exacerbating factor in his decline.

What it came down to, Judy realized, was that time was very much of the essence. She was fully aware of how months had been stretching into years. Sometimes, late at night when her children were asleep, she would sit in front of the fireplace staring at the flames as they ate away at the logs, and she would dream of the erosive effect that prison was having on her brother, grotesque dreams that left her in a panic. It didn't matter that everybody else seemed to have given up in despair —as though Joel's release was now a totally dead issue. She would silently rage at her Uncle Jack, believing he could have used his political clout to get Joel out had he wanted to. Whatever the truth of the matter, Joel had been in prison for eight years, he had twenty more to serve, and he was dying.

She *had* to do something!

She called her old friend Jerry Porter in Miami.
Look, she said, there's got to be someone who can do
this thing! Porter was not optimistic. He reminded her
of all the schemes she had tried, the money she had
spent. Hundreds of thousands of dollars. Hadn't she
gotten the message?

Please, she urged.

A few days later, Porter called back. There was
someone else he'd heard about. Not a Miami guy,
though. An independent guy. He didn't even know how
to get in touch with him. But he'd heard that this guy
was a friend of the folk-singer and movie actor, Burl
Ives. Judy should contact Burl Ives and ask to get in
touch with a man named Victor E. Stadter.

No, he didn't know Burl Ives's phone number.

Judy got moving immediately. When she finally got
Burl Ives on the phone, he allowed as how Vic was a
friend and told her he lived in Glendora, just outside
of Los Angeles.

From Porter to Ives to Stadter.

The ordeal of Joel David Kaplan was about to
enter its final phase.

He is a tall, well-built Californian with the style of
a Texan.

At fifty-one, he has a flaring reddish mustache,
curly red-brown hair, cowboy boots, and casual neat
clothes. Tough, resourceful, competent. Very friendly,
very candid. Direct frontal approach to all relationships,
business or social. Old-fashioned chivalry with woman,
especially when in distress.

He is the last of the rugged individualists. He be-
lieves in the right of a man to operate free of the
monstrous restrictions of bureaucracy. There are no
written contracts in Vic Stadter's business arrangements, for he mistrusts the world of brokers, agents,
lawyers. He prefers to make his arrangements verbally

and cement them with a handshake. He expects honesty from his associates, knowing he would never give anything less himself.

Vic Stadter is a smuggler.

Stadter was born in eastern Colorado, near a small town called Hoyt. His father, Elsworth Lentz Stadter, was an engineer, machinist, rancher, and inventor. Their heritage was German: Vic's grandfather had been a mercenary in a Prussian army group that came to America to fight for the Union Army in the Civil War, his two brothers with him. During the war, they had been captured by the South; after their release, they remained in America and started a freight service on wagons moving West. (Quipped smuggler Vic: "I am the last member of the family still in the transportation business.") His grandfather sired twelve children, the last being Vic's father; all did well for themselves. One became a Circuit Judge, one died rich in the San Francisco earthquake, one made a fortune digging gold in Alaska, one became a District Attorney in Oregon, and so on through the lot.

At thirteen Vic ran away from home "to see the bathing beauties of Florida." Arriving in Miami, he suffered his first loss of innocence: there were plenty of bathers but no beauties. He worked in Florida at fourteen, driving a truck from which he peddled beef he himself had killed, a moving butcher-shop that was also his sleeping quarters.

From his earliest boyhood, he wanted to fly. In 1939, he went to Canada to join the Royal Canadian Air Force, but was rejected because he was too young. Returning to California, he became a foreman in a machine shop, then joined the U.S. Navy hoping to go to sea, but was kept in his classification: machine-shop worker. So he went AWOL, and after he had done his time in the brig, he went AWOL again, and when they caught him he told the court-martial that he would continue to do the same until they sent him to

136

sea. Finally, they did, as a laundry-man aboard a destroyer. He made the North Atlantic run to Murmansk doing escort work, then all the way to the Pacific, finally serving antisubmarine duty in the Caribbean. After the war, he hauled whiskey in Oklahoma "because the stuff was in short supply." He turned $10 into $9500 in Las Vegas once on a lucky streak, then dropped a dime in a one-armed bandit and immediately hit the jackpot. "I knew it was my day. I should've stayed in town to run that dough into a million, but my partner forced me to leave. By God, when we hit the road I stuck out my thumb and stopped the first damn car that went by and he drove us straight to the door of my house in California!"

Luck. It is Stadter's way. The way he lives, he would have to be one of the luckiest men in history. Otherwise, he'd be dead. But there is a lot more to it than luck. Stadter is kind of a man who makes his own luck.

Stadter learned to run the Mexican border far better than any man had ever done. He became a specialist in Latin America, crossing the borders of a dozen countries literally hundreds of times, using all manner of ruses and modes of transportation, handling diverse contraband—from lobsters to linen.

There was a time in the late 1940's when he was trucking fresh coffee beans from Vera Cruz and he picked up a pet monkey to bring home to his wife. It turned out that everyone wanted to buy the monkey, not the coffee. Vic remembered that. Years later, when he was flying the border, he began what he later identified as his "monkey business," airfreighting cargos of capuchin and spider monkeys into the United States from Nicaragua "without benefit of Customs," having bribed the proper native official not only for permission to depart with his booty but also for assistance in the complex process of acquiring the animals. Vic was given a platoon of soldiers who went into the jungle with him and drove dozens out and into the nets of waiting henchmen. Back in the States, these smuggled animals were easily marketable, mostly to pet shops. He is an adventurer who lives with danger, most of which he has faced in all types of aircraft. Indeed, his face has been punished by accidents, his upper lip, now hidden by that huge mustache, scarred by repeated jolts. His nose, once curling "this way and that" over his face, was recently straightened by a skilled surgeon. And there are bones on his big rugged body that have broken and healed more than once.

He began his active romance with aviation just after World War II at a small airport at Vallejo, California, where he saw a beautiful new single-engine plane. He bought it immediately, took a dozen hours of flying lessons, then flew it all the way to Guatemala. One of the finest trouble pilots in America, Stadter was properly extolled in the June, 1969, issue of *Flight Magazine* as the man who flew 1,248 miles—from British Honduras to Brownsville, Texas—with one engine out on his Aero Commander. What awed this journal was that Stadter, impatient over the long delay that had kept him grounded in British Honduras while he waited for parts for his ailing engine, had simply unscrewed the inoperative propeller, tossed it in the back of his plane, and taken off on one engine. The magazine called it "adventurous death-defying flying," but could not figure out why any pilot would be in such a hurry in the first place. Vic, of course, had a perishable product to deliver, and it was essential to his code that he deliver it on time. "When you make a deal, you don't get paid to make excuses for not delivering. If you want a decent reputation, sometimes you have to take risks."

Over the years, the risks were sometimes excruciating, as when carrying a load of wrist watches from Switzerland, cigarette lighters from Japan, and linens from Ireland, he was ambushed by the opposition (read: authorities) at a rural airstrip in Central America. Just as he was revving up his engines, jeeploads of soldiers appeared and began firing into the cockpit of his Aero Commander. Vic threw himself on the cabin floor under a wash of bullets that tore apart the walls, then gunned the plane forward while operating the controls from the floor, unable to see a thing. "I lifted the plane by feel. When I dared to look back, I saw how close I must have come to a car they had stuck on the runway to block my takeoff."

Even his wife, Mary, has lived with danger in a marriage that included her companionship on a number of missions. Once, as the plane was running out of gas over a large expanse of water, she confronted all her worst fears accumulated over the years and, in a moment of some weakness, confessed them: "Well, this is it . . . We've had it now." Then, having said it, she immediately reversed herself, as any woman married to Stadter would have to do: "But, that's okay, Vic; really, everything is going to turn out fine."

And so it did, of course. Land appeared in the distance as the engine spluttered its dying gasps, and they glided in for a soft landing on the beach. Even as he landed, Vic was figuring how much time he had to get gas before the tide came in.

Vic dismisses his lack of fear with a shrug. "When you're in trouble, you have too much to do to get scared. You've got to save yourself. You don't have time to think of the dangers."

Over the years, Stadter has performed a variety of jobs, some as safe as driving the giant statue of the lady identified with *Myra Breckenridge* on a three-week cross-country promotional tour for the motion picture made from that novel; or the formation of his backyard business of manufacturing portable cement barbecue pits.

But mostly, he is a man who has constantly cheated death and Customs, and kept up a feud with the growing bureaucracy of the Federal Aviation Agency. He pathologically despises those "feeders at the public trough" who live by rote and manual, and who love to encumber in red tape anyone who chooses a more venturesome career. Vic has missed few opportunities to display his contempt. Once, for example, he was preparing to land on a Florida strip when his radio broke down, so he sent the required landing communication to the control tower by dropping a note on its deck contained in a paper bag weighted with a dried-up peanut butter and jelly sandwich. That did it. A highly insulted young bureaucrat pored over the FAA code book and compiled some seventy-five separate violations supposedly committed by Vic. "It looked like a Chinese Army laundry list," he quips, pointing out that only a couple of the charges were ever made to stick.

Then, in 1962, the government came up with something that did stick. As Stadter tells it, "I was set up by federal agents on a conspiracy rap." Shaky though the charges were—they hung on the word of a lone informant—the government rammed through a conviction, and Stadter was sentenced to eight years in the Federal Penitentiary at Lewisburg (he served five) "for nothing more than revenge against a successful individualist."

His resentments against bureaucratic authority stewed during those five years, and when he regained his freedom, the only thing he had learned from his punishment was that the United States Government was not always the servant of its citizens. To Vic Stadter, it became the symbol of repression, of the curtailment of individual freedom, of the corruption of the democratic institutions he had been taught to believe in. From such a vantage point, it was only a short leap to the conviction that all other governments were doubtlessly much the same.

So, when he heard Judy Kaplan Dowis appeal for his help in liberating her brother, it was more than the possibility of making a large dollar that lured him. This was a job he could enjoy, a form of revenge, as it were, an affirmation of his beliefs. As he would put it later on: "Hell, I would've taken him out for nothing!"

This from a man with a price on his head in Mexico of 1,000,000 pesos.

20

Vic Stadter's meeting with Joel was considerably less than dramatic, for neither found the other particularly inspiring. Vic was brought to Acatitla by Irma and Judy, introduced as a friend of the family whom Irma lovingly referred to as El Cangrejo Viejo—"The Old Crab." Joel was cordial, but indifferent. He had already met with too many would-be rescuers to have faith in another. All he could see was another nameless face from Judy's stable of oddballs—and one could hardly blame him for his doubts.

Though Vic had been through many prisons in his day—both from inside and from out—he was hard put to recall ever confronting a prisoner as sickly and beaten as Joel. "He had a chalky color that people like to associate with convicts in solitary. No fresh air, no sunlight. This man looked like he had one foot in the grave. There was even a musty smell to him."

Vic saw a monkey-barrel full of problems.

Joel was sick, depressed, nervous. That was one problem.

Another was Joel's propensity for playing the patsy, dreaming up and submitting to an unending stream of preposterous escape schemes. At their meeting, Vic listened with dismay as Joel related the most recent of

142

these aborted escapes. According to the plan, Joel was to have hidden behind a pile of laundry loaded in a delivery truck and, with the bribed help of some prison laundry workers and the truck's driver, be driven to freedom. Inevitably, someone copped out, someone else talked, and everyone kept the bribe money.

Joel had already paid out too much money too loosely, and that was yet another problem because it violated Vic's proven philosophy of the bribe. Vic was the master of the bribe and he knew all its nuances. A bribe was to be treated like an art form in much the same delicate way a diamond cutter uses his skill. An indiscriminate bribe was a crime in itself, for it tended to jar the sacred process for others. But there was also human nature; one just doesn't blow up a free-flowing well. "The more money he gave away to get out," Stadter states, "the more the people he gave it to wanted to keep him in."

At the time of their meeting, Joel was well into another escape scheme, this one at least as costly as the others. Typically, it began in the dormitory shower room and reached fruition in the machine shop toilet.

In prison, there is a lot more talk about escape than the number of actual attempts would justify—like adolescent boys talking about the girls they've seduced. In Mexican prisons, there are even fewer attempts, not because security is so tight, but because many Mexican prisoners are not oriented toward escape. They're simply not that eager for their cherished freedom—primarily, one assumes, because their existence in jail is not that much worse than their existence on the outside. As the old U.S. Army expression puts it, you get three hots and a cot. For many of them, the denial of these basic requirements in their free life was what brought them to jail in the first place.

Nonetheless, escapes, like sex, make interesting

prison conversation, and a man's concern for the subject is respected as a demonstration of *machismo*. Joel always made it a point not to talk about escapes at all, even in jest. It was a sort of discipline; the less said, the better. But he always kept his ears open.

So, when someone began making jokes in the shower room about riding out of prison hidden in one of the trailers being constructed in the prison metal shop, Joel started thinking.

At Santa Marta, another American inmate named John Church ran the metal shop, having won for himself a first-rate flim-flam with the Mexico City branch of an American trailer company. Church's tour of duty in Mexican prisons did not begin so smoothly: he had suffered the seemingly medieval punishment of being welded into his first jail cell at Lecumberri prison. Church was there because he had killed a policeman with a karate chop, a felony he compounded by bribing his Lecumberri jailers with "hot" American Express traveler's checks. That little trick merited him the welding treatment, a punishment cruel and inhuman enough to precipitate the intervention of the American Embassy. Transferred to Santa Marta, Church's fortunes began to rise. There, he had made a home for himself: with a crew of prison labor and a tidy subcontracting operation, he turned out forty-foot trailers far more cheaply than any legitimate business could, gaining a substantial profit for himself and the prison authorities he kept on his payroll. A private business inside the prison walls.

Joel decided to approach him with a private business matter of his own: a false front built on the trailer bulkhead, just wide enough for a small man. An easy job for an experienced metal worker, and, since the trailers were so long, the added foot or two on the bulkhead would never be detected.

A simple plan. So simple it was absolutely perfect.

It was so perfect, even El Cangrejo Viejo had to admit it could work.

The trouble was, Joel couldn't get John Church alone: there was always someone around him in his shop. He finally hit a lucky moment just as Church was going to the toilet in the rear of his shop. Joel found him sitting on the throne, unappreciative of the intrusion.

"Church, I can make you some extra money."

"How much?"

"Let's say 75,000 pesos."

"Make it 100,000. Then I'll think about it."

"All right, 100,000."

He really didn't have to tell Church what he wanted. Details were thrashed out in subsequent meetings. Church allowed as how he could do the job in a few hours, after a trailer was allegedly finished. He would have to do it alone, in the evening when the shop was closed—not difficult for him since he lived in a special room over the shop. He would use the next trailer to come off the line; when it was finished, he'd get in touch with Joel. On a night they'd agree on in advance, he'd build the compartment in which Joel would stand, hidden, pressed close to the bulkhead. It would be picked up by a tractor from the trailer company and taken a few miles away for a test run on a special open lot normally used for parking. Testing there was not an unfamiliar procedure. All Church had to do was call the prison Chief of Vigilance and get permission.

El Cangrejo Viejo would be there waiting.

The way Joel read Church, however, he was the type who could easily take the money and betray him. He might even send Joel out in the bulkhead and have him captured, perhaps even killed. Joel therefore insisted that the man accompany him, knowing Vic could handle him if anything went wrong. When the switch was made from trailer to car, then and only then would

Church get the balance of the payment, the second 50,000 pesos.

It was a fine set-up, but as Joel had learned by then, no better than the man who was to execute it. As was customary, Church wanted his money in advance, to be delivered to his wife's bank in Mexico City, and so it was arranged, the money coming from Judy's account. It was now simply a question of timing.

But Church began to stall.

Vic Stadter could smell a live rat long before most people would smell a dead one. He had never met John Church. In fact, after that first visit to Acatitla to meet Joel, he never went back and never would. ("I had my share of prison life at Lewisburg. I'd just as soon keep my ass outside of those gates.") But when John Church began stalling, Vic knew there would be no end to it. To Vic, the secret word was timing. He could never tolerate delays. As soon as an action was delayed, he would bet it would never work. Delays indicated vacillation and weakness. The reasons did not interest him. Whatever the reasons, they opened the door to failure. Church had told Joel that the guards were coming around more often than usual, looking at the trailers, but Vic didn't believe it. At this first level of stalling, Vic knew the deal was not going to go through, and any further payments would be chasing good money after bad.

He immediately wired Judy to have payment stopped on the check he had delivered to Church's wife, who lived in Mexico City. He followed that up with a phone call to Sausalito, only to learn that no action had yet been taken on the telegram. It was the sort of failure that Vic found terribly distressing.

Shortly thereafter, Vic learned that his suspicions had been accurate. Church had, indeed, refused to make that secret compartment in the trailer and the check had not been stopped in time. The Mexico City bank

146

manager had cleared payment claiming that he had not received the stop-notice until a day too late, that apparently it had been delayed in transit, or misplaced in his bank offices.

What Vic did not know until weeks later was that the bank manager was Mrs. John Church's uncle.

Said Joel: "It was a miserable ending to a fine idea. Not so much because of the money I'd spent or the bad feeling of the betrayal. What I regretted most was the failure of a damned good plan. I would dream about that plan for a long time. In many ways, it was the best plan I ever had."

21 Vic Stadter's first full assignment in the escapes of Joel Kaplan would be, to put it gently, less than satisfying. An assignment—that was all it was—in which he was no more than appendage to a plan he had no hand in organizing. What he liked least were the unknown factors over which he had no control, a predictable reaction from one whose nature dictated that he be in full command from the inception.

Still, it was far from a total loss, for with it he proved, once again, what a remarkable operative he had in the man known as Pussy.

Pussy was Patrick Lyle Lipscomb; how he had acquired that nickname was his secret. A Californian in his mid-forties, Pussy had known Vic more than twenty years. They'd met at a time when Pussy had been selling produce. Vic had watched him operate and liked his style. Vic Stadter knew a good man when he met one, and, needing expertise in various food products he wanted to transport, he took Pussy with him to develop his burgeoning Mexican business.

"Pussy is one of those men with what seem like unlimited abilities," Vic says of him. "A perfect operative who can handle himself in different languages in proper dialects. He could pass as a native almost anywhere he went with that remarkable combination of color, style, eye shape, hair—he would blend right into the scenery like a man who had never been any place else. His father was Portuguese, his mother was French, and nobody knows what combination preceded them. He's light enough to be white and dark enough to be black. If there was a problem with blacks, he'd move right in among them, creating no sense of racial animosity no matter what his allegiance. He'd be accepted. The same with Chicanos. It was as if he belonged to them all. He knows when to talk and when not to. He could keep silent for days, waiting patiently and stoically in any situation no matter how critical. He'd know exactly when to make his move. I could not function without Pussy in Mexico."

Vic brought Pussy to Mexico City in 1970 to assist in the getaway operations. Before a year was out, Pussy would make over twenty trips to Mexico City as his representative, using his remarkable acceptability to gain unlimited access through the prison gate at Acatitla.

"He was so good, even Joel came to trust him."

Pussy was assigned to bird dog the plan that Joel had been working on for months—a transfer from Acatitla to the penitentiary at Cuernavaca. The problem, as Joel repeatedly petitioned the authorities, was primarily medical. He needed the cleaner atmosphere of the Cuernavaca mountains to recover from his frequent bouts with hepatitis and the over-all debilitation of his body that had resulted. There was no question about the extent of his sickness. "You see that look and you never forget it," Vic said. "You see a man who knows he's in trouble and it scares the bejesus out of him. He talks in a way that don't always make sense. It ain't his head that's talking, it's the shakes."

A transfer for reasons of health, yes. But it is also

noteworthy that Cuernavaca was the ultimate in mini-mum security prisons. There, prisoners were permitted to go into town, enjoying the sort of freedom that could be considered comparable to that of an American prep school student. A prison without a gate, as it were.

It was an ideal place for Joel Kaplan.

Vic was also aware—as was Joel—that the very transfer that was so resourcefully designed to save his life might just as resourcefully be designed to kill him. Any time such a transfer is made, the man being moved becomes extremely vulnerable. To get a prisoner past the prison gate requires bribes. Those same bribes mean that, once on the road, the prisoner is a candidate for ambush. On the road to Cuernavaca, there is a turn-off into what is frequently referred to as "the gravel pit." More than gravel fills this pit; it is also the reposi-tory of organic matter—human bones. All too often, the transfer car is driven off the highway onto the dirt road leading to the gravel pit, the prisoner is pulled out of the car at gunpoint and told to run for his life. It is called *ley de fugas*—"the flight." So he runs—at least until the bullets slam into his back. Another prisoner shot trying to escape. What better way for a well-bribed official to protect himself from the accusation that he'd been a well-bribed official?

This was what Vic saw as the inevitable conse-quence of a corrupt bureaucratic system. "If you bribe a man to violate his responsibilities, he is no longer trustworthy to anyone. He is apt to betray you just as he betrayed the people he was working for in the first place. He is a tainted man who lives by being a fraud."

The transfer had, nonetheless, to be attempted.

Vic was skeptical. He told himself it was his own vanity that made him cool to the plan, that he never trusted what he himself did not control, that he'd better go about the business of arranging for the proper escort and stop belittling the deal just because someone else had arranged it. He had been informed of all the money that had changed hands, several thousand dollars passed out to Mexican officials, mostly medics in the health services, bribed to report that Joel's physical condition was, indeed, a very dangerous one. There were others who had been handed money and they told Joel, then Vic, that the orders for the transfer would be called through very soon and that Vic would be notified as to the exact time of departure. So he set up a procedure to insure maximum protection. Pussy would be at the wheel of a car waiting outside the prison gate, ready to follow the official car as it passed through the gate, staying right on its tail in a way that immediately declared its intent. A second car would be stationed down the road less than a mile from the prison in case a problem developed with the first; this second car would be loaded with the heavy artillery. Vic would be in the second car, prepared for any eventuality. "If I saw evidence that there was going to be trouble I would not hesitate to move in and snatch Joel right out of their hands."

Then the call came through. Joel was to be transferred on the night of January 16, 1971, at 10:00, an hour that did not sit well with Vic since night offered far more concealment for ambush than day. As an extra precaution, he had a highpowered spotlight mounted on his car, and every man was armed with the best flashlight available. And, from the time the last contact was made with Joel just prior to the evening check-in, Pussy waited in a car outside the gate to be certain the officials did not jump their own gun.

Vic and his cars were posted and ready, but no one went in or out of the prison gate throughout the long night.

At a few minutes after 8 A.M., Irma was called by an official with whom she had been conducting these negotiations; he reported that the transfer had been made successfully and that the balance of the money, $80,000, should be delivered to him immediately. She

151

was startled by the call, for she had sat up all night vainly waiting for Vic to report in with the same news. Now, she immediately phoned Vic, reaching him at his hotel just as he came in from his long vigil and relaying the message. Vic, who had a man ready with the money, told her that to his knowledge no such transfer had been made, but to be certain, he suggested she go to Santa Marta and see if Joel were still there.

No sooner had he hung up when his phone rang again. "It was those same officials. They wanted the money. I said, sure. But I was going to stall them until I heard from Irma."

For the first time, Irma was frightened.

This had all begun on the highest levels in the Mexican government—she had herself visited Moya Palencia, the acting head of the secretariat responsible for the bureaucratic details attendant to prison transfers. Palencia had in turn referred her to those subordinates in the secretariat's echelons who could fulfill her request. It had seemed so smooth. But something had gone wrong. She knew it.

Although she had long since become accustomed to disappointments, this time she was keenly tuned to the dangers. She told herself that she was worried unnecessarily, but as she drove hurriedly to Santa Marta, she fantasized a series of frightening images of Joel being marched out on foot and brutally murdered in the night.

At the gate, there was a new guard, someone she had never seen before, and a ghoulish chill raced through her. She struggled to maintain whatever poise she could muster in the face of this new obstacle, believing that only by her serenity would this off-hours visit be permitted, but she could not act the role and felt herself crumbling under a new wave of panic. By some marvelous irony, it was her rising hysteria that induced the guard to let her pass.

Yes, Joel was there. He had heard nothing. No one had contacted him. He had passed the same semi-sleepless night that had typified the preceding weeks.

When Vic heard Irma's report, his scowl was as predictable as the validity of his original doubts. This was to be another cop-out deal, arranged by amateurs, corrupted by thieves, and paid for by suckers. Several more phone calls from the thieves had come through while he'd waited for Irma. They kept asking him to come down to their office, they wanted to talk to him. And when he called them back after hearing from Irma, they seemed even more urgent.

"What for?" he replied, thinking that, since Joel was still in Santa Marta, there was no further business to be transacted.

"Then I got the message. They wanted to work a deal with me. I was to give them half the money, $40,000, and Joel would never know why the transfer never came through. I was to keep the remaining $40,000 and go back to California. Jesus H. Christ. I laughed. If I wanted to betray Joel I could just take the $80,000 I had in the next room and go. What in hell did I have to split it with them for!"

He could not resist railing at them, furious at this corruption of what he'd assumed to be a legitimate bribe. As he saw it, these officials were violating an agreement as binding as a notarized contract.

He told Irma there was not going to be a transfer. He knew that now, and she had to agree with him. In fact, she said she had doubted it from the beginning. She had gone along with it because of Joel—he had believed them.

Vic understood. He had heard enough about Joel

during these last few weeks to know a man who was beginning to crack, who was going to believe only what he wanted to believe, a man who could no longer see an unhappy truth if his life depended on it. He had been sitting there too long. "Joel was so intent on getting out you could've sold him a toy balloon and told him it was magic, that all he had to do was blow it up and hang on and it would fly him out."

Again, Vic was right. Joel insisted that the transfer was still in the works, demanding reassurance that Vic would be there to protect him. Reluctantly, Vic agreed to do this. Yes, he would keep watch at the gate for a few days more.

Meanwhile, Vic did some digging. He was not surprised to find out that the officials had been ousted from office months before and were no longer officially anything. They could not have arranged Joel's transfer even had they wanted to.

154

22 Judy was discouraged. It was as if a little piece of her soul was getting chewed away as each failure was reported to her. She had let over a quarter of a million dollars run through her account and none of it had turned out to be payment for honest, intelligent work. This was the most harrowing part. It wasn't the money; she had never really cared about the money. It was that brutal breach of simple humanity that, with so few exceptions, ran through these years that hit her hardest. Everybody thought it was okay to cheat everybody else. The time of the great rip-off. Everybody was fair game. The more you needed help, the more vulnerable you were, the more vultures came to tear you apart.

So she sat in her Sausalito mansion listening to Vic's tale and she could feel those claws in her flesh again. For a moment she could not cope with the anguish, but she did not want to cry in front of this man. Not that he would have been critical, it just didn't go with the way she wanted him to think of her. She rushed out of the room as she choked back tears. When she returned a few minutes later, having washed her face, lit a cigarette, put on a smile, he had not moved except to pour her a drink. He would make no comment, she knew. She sat down again and dared to look him in the eye.

"So how's the weather down there?" She was play-acting now.

"Sunny."

"Well, that's nice."

"Naah. It heats up the stink."

She laughed and he joined her, and suddenly it was time for levity. He took advantage of that. He told her that he had only one real complaint with this deal—his need for secrecy kept him out of the whorehouses. In the past, he had made phone calls from hotel rooms, even met in an office every once in a while, but all the big deals were consummated in whorehouses. The way he saw it, if you end up doing business in a man's office, you've sunk pretty low in the world. He had become the King of the Cat Houses, knowing all the best ones in every town in Latin America. They weren't just sex palaces; they were like fine hotels with good rooms, baths, fine eating places, appealing bars. All the best people went to them. But in this matter with Joel, he had to stay clear of them; even cat house walls have eyes and ears.

Then, finishing his drink, he refilled his glass from the bottle of Old Smuggler's Judy kept for him, knowing it was the only Scotch he drank. Judy laughed again, enjoying the exuberance of this hard-drinking man, enjoying, too, the wry humor that made him so loyal to his brand. But he was serious now, and it stopped her.

"I'll get him out for you, Judy."

She looked up at him, so struck by the certainty of it she had to laugh again.

"How?"

"I'll buy him out. It'll cost you, but only if I can swing it."

"How much?"

"I'll let you know," he said.

Within a week, Vic was back in Mexico City, this time on his own, the project solidly in his hands. The way he read it, the simplest way was to buy Joel out with straight cash, hit the right officials this time and make a deal. This was Mexico and he'd never heard of a prisoner who couldn't be sprung with the right sum of money.

He began talking to people he knew around the Mexican capital, important people with the best contacts, letting it be known he had lots of money to offer.

Then he heard the bad news: "This Kaplan business. If I were you, I'd forget it. You can't buy him out!"

He was stunned. His contacts were totally reliable, he had worked with them in the past; they knew where the bodies were buried, they knew it all. "They told me about punks who got busted for dealing big in heroin and other hard stuff, how the United States Government itself had pressured the Mexicans to put them in jail and keep them there, but my contacts had gotten them out; it had merely cost a bit more. But with Kaplan, the door was shut. I was told 'No matter who you get to go along with you, no matter how much you pay, there'll be somebody else with better contacts and more money working to keep him in.' "

He went back to his hotel, contemplating what his next move ought to be. As he walked through the lobby, he was aware that a man had come up beside him, a stout, dark man in a clean white shirt, no tie, his eyes hidden by sunglasses; he might have been a Mexican, Vic didn't know for sure.

"Stadter . . ."

Vic stopped in the middle of the lobby as the man indicated he wished to talk. Could they sit for a minute or two in that corner sofa?

The dialogue was right out of John Le Carré.

"Mr. Stadter, they tell me to treat you with great respect . . ."

Vic was conscious that this stranger had not only

known him by his real name, but had pronounced it correctly, a rare occurrence at first meeting. Most people try to sound every letter. Actually, he pronounced it "Stodder."

"We are aware that you have the resources to get your man out," the man continued, withdrawing a pack of cigarettes from his shirt pocket, the matches tucked neatly inside the cellophane wrapper. He offered Vic a smoke. Declined.

". . . So we want to make you a proposition—*if* you succeed in this."

It was a switch, all right. Vic had trouble with that last line. The man was obviously letting it sink in, taking a ludicrously long drag on his cigarette.

"What do you mean?" Vic asked.

"We'll give you fifty grand if you throw him back into Mexico."

Vic was amused now, though he was fully conscious of how serious this was. He looked hard at the man, so careful to come unarmed—or so it was deliberately made to appear—and he speculated on the possibilities of breaking the pudgy arm right there in the lobby in hopes of getting him to reveal his sponsors, knowing how stupid that would be even if he could get away with it. There was probably nothing the man could tell him, he was nothing more than a messenger, not even an operative, just some fat punk they'd hired and told exactly what to say. They make contact but they're covered ten layers thick, no one could ever find out what the real source was. CIA? Mexican Secret Service? Uncle Jack? Or somebody else?

Vic got up from the sofa without another word, walked directly across the lobby to the elevator. "I thought, shit on this hotel, I might just as well have gone to a whorehouse."

23 In the early afternoon of June 10, 1971, a slight, dark, inconspicuous man we'll call Alfred Court arrived at the Mexico City International Airport from New York carrying a small flight bag containing only a few simple personal effects. He told Customs officials that he had come to Mexico City to visit friends and that he intended to stay only a few days, exactly as his sparse luggage suggested. He was immediately passed without further question, and Court proceeded to the taxi stand, directing the driver to take him to the Hotel del Prado.

If the Customs officials had examined him thoroughly, they might have discovered a highly provocative if bewildering curiosity: Court was wearing a neatly trimmed black wig—not in itself startling; what lay under the wig was something else again, for Court had the identical hairdo the wig was so perfectly designed to imitate.

Had this phenomenon been discovered, any Mexican official worth his bribable soul would have asked the inevitable question: why would a man wear a wig exactly like his natural hair?

The answer would have truly excited them: the man we are calling Alfred Court was, by profession, a make-up artist and occasional operative of the man

159

whose real name was Victor E. Stadter. In this instance, he was indeed in Mexico City for a few days, hopefully no more, but not "to visit friends." He was there to arrange an identity crisis at the Santa Marta prison, as a result of which Joel David Kaplan would become a free man.

This time, it was Stadter who conceived the idea for Joel's escape; since he could not buy him out, he decided to walk him out. Pussy already had on the payroll two key guards at the prison hospital and one señorita who worked at the prison entrance during visiting hours. The wig on Court's head was made by specialists in New York for the munificent sum of $700, tailored as closely as possible to the combined specifications of both Court's and Kaplan's headsize, fortunately of similar structure.

The plan was simple enough. As Vic said, all good plans had to be simple. Court would enter the Santa Marta prison with "a friend," the operative named Pussy, ostensibly to visit the prisoner Joel Kaplan. Inside Joel's hospital room, unseen by anyone, Court would remove the wig, place it on Joel's head, perform a rapid make-up job on Joel's face with the tools of his trade (which he had hidden on his person), give Joel his own clothes—a complete switch of appearance that would leave Kaplan looking exactly like Court. When finished, Pussy would drug and bind Court to make it appear that he was a victim rather than the perpetrator.

Joel and Pussy would then walk out of the prison as innocently as they had allegedly entered it.

As Vic figured it, Court could not be held responsible since no one would be able to prove anything against him. Indeed, what evidence could there possibly be? Joel and wig, the only evidence of collusion, would be a thousand miles away. Court would certainly be held in jail overnight, but Vic had an attorney ready to move in on the following day to demand his release.

160

The only danger appeared to lie in the outside chance that Joel would be stopped at the gate by some suspicious official who noticed something awry. Court himself advised Vic of the possibilities. No make-up artist could conceal some identifiable quirk of body movement, a telltale cant of head or type of stride. Seen from the rear or side, it was sometimes a dead giveaway. It was definitely a possibility—even though they had, in part, protected themselves with those bribes. But if Joel were stopped at the gate and the wig removed, and if Court were nabbed in Joel's hospital cell . . .

For a man like Alfred Court, it was a very reasonable gamble. He had worked for Vic enough times to trust his judgment on such matters. He would be paid for his talent and the dangers, $2500 for a few days work, plus expenses, plus a few reasonably hot meals in the not-so-chic resort of Santa Marta Acatitla. What's more, he could always tell the story to his grandchildren.

The plan was ready to go when suddenly, unpredictably, Joel was transferred out of the hospital and back to his prison cell "for reasons of adequate health" —or so Vic was informed by Pussy through one of the bribed guards.

A crusher, as they say. More than any other factor, Vic was sensitive to the problems that result from delay. He knew one thing for sure: as rapidly as possible he had to get Joel back into the hospital, for this was not a scheme that could be worked out of the turmoil of Joel's dormitory.

The man who could bring that off was some 1800 miles away in the city of Los Angeles. Knowing no Mexican physician he could trust with so delicate an assignment, Vic immediately hopped a plane for Los Angeles. The Los Angeles M.D. was another associate of Vic's, a talented man in his field, a genuine healer with an imaginative mind.

Later that evening, Vic joined the doctor in the privacy of his study. There, they pored over the proper medical books on tropical diseases, finally deciding on a fairly commonplace one whose symptoms were relatively easy to duplicate in the body of the now adequately healthy Joel Kaplan.

Inside of a few hours, the doctor had put together the ingredients of a pill that would give Joel an attack of shakes and fever strikingly similar to a vicious case of malaria. Vic returned to Mexico City with this magic pellet, which Pussy immediately brought to the prisoner with instructions to ingest it then and there so that it might take effect by morning. Because the pill's effects would last only twenty-four hours, they planned to make their move on the following day—with the aid of a few recuperative pellets of aspirin.

Joel, meanwhile, had been hit hard by this bewildering twist of fate. That his escape had been foiled by this "adequacy of health" was a brutally savage blow for he had never been sicker over a longer period than in these last six months. He lay in his cell letting it all swirl around him, suddenly hating the jabbering of his cellmate, the irrepressible Venezuelan Carlos Antonio Contreras Castro, who seemed overly pleased at his return to the dormitory.

Joel had reached the point where his mind could no longer tolerate defeat and remain sane. He had so determinedly set his sights on escape as his only way of survival that prison had become a menace to sanity itself, or so he had begun to interpret it.

He would wake up in the middle of the night bathed in sweat, not from nightmarish dreams of fantasy, but from a sudden glimpse at the grotesque reality of his plight. He was locked up tighter than a drum and no attack on the system of Mexican justice was going to get him out, no lawyers named Nizer or Velasquez, no newspaper publicity, no force he could conceive of was strong enough to withstand the power of his oppressors.

Time had seriously compromised his faith. He could literally feel the power of those lined up against him. They had him trapped and as he plotted to get out, they kept plotting to keep him in. He even made jokes about it with Castro, who accused him of paranoia. Said Joel: "You'd be paranoid too if people were always plotting against you." It was fine that he could laugh about it, but pain was beginning to choke his laughter, and as his mind had begun to suffer from it, so it was with his body. He'd go to bed sick and wake up sicker. He drank to ease his anguish, then suffered the consequences of his excesses. He did not know how to control it any more.

Now here was another bottle of Bacardi when he needed it, so he drank, but his mind was tuned to only one direction: that hospital cell. He had so fully prepared himself for this escape with the make-up artist, building that marvelously exciting anticipation of success—this time, yes, *this time* it was going to work, nothing could possibly fail *this time*—that he refused to let go of it.

His will was enormous, his motivations unstoppable. So Joel David Kaplan willed himself sick. Inside of four hours, he was sweating with a fever, throwing up food, then blood, then suffering chills, sicker than Castro had even seen him.

This was the way Pussy discovered him when he brought the magic pill from the doctor in Los Angeles.

Joel was back in the hospital, but three days had elapsed since the appointed time of deliverance. Vic was wary. The master, always scrupulously organized, sent Pussy into Santa Marta on the day before the plan was to be reactivated. A routine check on all concerned, just to be sure that the wheels would turn properly. What happened was a shocker: everyone at the front gate had heard something in one form or another, relating to one prisoner or another, but especially to Joel. A special guard was being posted to tug at all suspicious hairdos. In fact, every visitor who wasn't totally bald was going to be challenged.

Said Pussy: "You couldn't have had a better publicity job if you'd had it on TV."

Vic would never know exactly who had leaked it, though there had been touchy moments several days before in Irma's apartment when they'd been laughing at the prospects, their voices rising foolishly, carelessly, and they could hear others stirring in the adjacent apartment behind thin, porous walls. They'd quieted immediately, but was the damage done at that instant? Did someone hear just enough to have some fun of his own?

Whatever. The time factor had beaten him again.

The Great Walkout had ended without a step.

24

It was Vic's turn for depression. He had been through twenty-five years of all sorts of adventures, win some, lose some, but especially this time he did not like the taste of defeat. He was a man who could fly by the seat of his pants, a man with a special feel for things, and suddenly the feel was a nasty one. He was a hard-nosed practical man, free of all forms of bullshit and artifice and superstition, but it crossed his mind that maybe he'd gotten himself into one of those doomed things, that maybe Joel was a born loser. But he had promised Judy that he would get Joel out and he had never gone back on a promise. It wasn't ritual or anything like that. He'd never sworn a pledge to it or made a New Year's resolution. It was simply the way he was. He had promised because he believed he could do it. He had accepted the job because he wanted to do it. There was no time for other considerations.

But now the big question was: how?

Joel was drunk again, but he wasn't laughing. He was angry and he was scared. Castro was yapping about how life went in cycles, how you had to submit to these tests of fate because it was all part of some grand plan that had something to do with the moon and tides and the month in which you were born. Joel had heard all that before in one form or another, the prison world was full of mystics. At the moment, it bothered him to hear it, not because he didn't believe it but because he knew that Castro didn't believe it. It was merely Castro's need to talk; he had to talk all the time, it was part of his pathology. Joel had once kidded him about it, asking how, in God's name, he had found time to get into trouble. And Castro, the convicted forger, had replied that it had come about during a week when he'd had this awful case of laryngitis.

He liked Castro. If one filtered the nonsense from his conversation, what remained could justify the torrent. And in back of it all, the man was decent. Joel knew he could trust him. But now Joel was drunk and, in the face of all those words, he began to question that trust. Castro knew about the make-up artist and the walkout. Needing his help, Joel had had to tell him. Could it be that Castro had leaked it? Was it his big mouth that had spoken a few too many words? Was this another instance where Joel had been too trusting?

Drunk or sober, he knew the symptoms. The paranoia again. He took another drink and fought it off. He looked at Castro and he saw a friend who, in his own garrulous way, was trying to ease his agony.

And Joel thought, my God, if I don't get out of here I'll die.

"It used to be a more or less occasional thought in my mind. I'd go through periods when I'd concentrate on escape ideas; like a scientist working on a cure for some disease, it was the center of my thoughts, but not to the exclusion of all others. I was involved in other things, I kept up on my reading, Marx, Fanon, Regis Debray, many periodicals from all over, newspapers. But in those last months, all that seemed to slip away from me. I had become so single-mindedly intent on escaping that it had made me sick. I simply could not

166

think of anything else. One starts dreaming that there's a deep hole in the floor and it's so dark you can't see it—if you take a step, any step, you just might fall in it, you don't know what to do. . . .

"I was drunk, but I didn't want to listen to Castro anymore, so I got up from my bed and said I was going to take a walk in the yard, alone. He thought I was crazy—it was the wrong time of day for that, the middle of the afternoon in bright sunlight. I'd get my head blown off by that sun, he said. I didn't care. Maybe that's what I needed.

"So I went out and walked around the patio. The sun made my head spin, just as I knew it would; I felt giddy and then stupid, and the more I walked, the less important anything seemed.

"And then, standing there like a drunken boob, in the middle of that yard, it hit me, the weirdest idea of all, yet unmistakably the simplest:

"I could fly out of here in a helicopter."

Part
ESCAPE
Four

25 Vic was impressed. The minute he'd heard of Joel's suggestion, he sensed it could work. All the fundamentals were there: an inner courtyard without supervision, accessible to Joel at specific hours. All Vic had to do was get a helicopter in there and take Joel out. There were, as he put it, "only thirty or forty things that might go wrong."

The trouble was the familiar one: the time element. It would take time to organize and time would breed leaks. He decided to keep as much information as possible out of Mexico City in general and from Joel Kaplan in particular. Joel would have to sweat it out in blind faith that Vic was making progress.

Vic had already made modifications in Joel's original concept, which had been that a helicopter would fly over the courtyard, drop a ladder which Joel would grab and be lifted up and away. The helicopter, Vic said, would have to land inside the prison, and Joel would have to get inside the way passengers normally do. Just how that could be accomplished was one of Vic's problems.

There was also the question of cost. It would be expensive. They'd need a helicopter that could operate at Santa Marta's 7600-foot altitude with its very thin air. Vic presented the problem to Judy. She didn't know if she had enough money, but she would find a way of getting it. If Vic thought the idea was promising, that was good enough for her. In fact, she went beyond that—she liked the idea. For the first time, she was sparked by something, this whole notion of plucking Joel out of that prison and flying away with him.

"Where did he get such a beautiful idea?" she asked.

Vic replied that Joel had said something about medical rescues in Vietnam, helicopters taking the wounded out of enemy territory and flying them back to base hospitals. (Later, newspapers would say Joel had seen such a rescue done by the FBI on the weekly TV series and he had related it to his own predicament. Joel's comment to that was: "Nonsense, I never watched TV. And if I had, I'd certainly never have watched a show about the FBI.")

"I'd like to go along for the ride," said Judy.

The simple act of flying him out was going to be the end of a complex organizational process. To begin with, Vic needed a helicopter pilot.

Old airplane pilots were a dime-a-dozen to Vic, but he was sorely lacking in trustworthy operatives who could fly choppers. They were a young man's ballgame. It's the kids who fly choppers (not airplanes), the way kids ride cycles (not cars). Veteran pilots generally have nothing to do with them. They don't even consider them aircraft—just big dumb toys, floppy and unpredictable. Said Vic: "Nobody'd ever heard of the damn things until the Korean War." He hated helicopters.

"It left me in trouble, all right. You just don't go around to any helicopter pilot you might run into and say 'Mister, I've got this guy I want to spring from a Mexican pen and I need your help.' You've got to know the man first; he's got to be someone you can trust, someone you know well enough to work with. And, as soon as one guy you don't know turns you down knowing what you want him to do, your whole project is in security trouble."

In desperation, he decided to learn to fly a helicopter himself. And since he was pressed for time, he signed up with two different schools, doubling his instruction period in hopes of splitting the learning time in half.

It went badly.

"I had too many things on my mind, too many details to worry about. I was thinking, if I could learn to handle that chopper, I could work the whole escape with only one other man plus my daughter, Mary Jane. That way, we would have a real tight ship, no chance of leaks. But I needed time. A month, say, and I would've been able to pull it off. But Joel was having it rough. I mean, he was really screaming about getting out, he just couldn't wait any longer.

"So I contacted an old pilot friend, Cotton. Cotton was my man. He'd never flown choppers either, but the way I figured him, he could learn to fly anything no matter what, all it needed was a rubber band to wind up the propeller."

He was a Texan named Harvey Orville Dail, nicknamed "Cotton" by his father when he was a towheaded boy. He was of Irish–Cherokee Indian stock, the Irish side having arrived in the United States five generations before. Like Vic, he had grown up into a rugged, spirited, resourceful man "doing one thing or another and seldom the same thing twice." Most recently, a crop duster from the air, a job he liked only because it meant flying.

Cotton was in his early forties, big and tough, with thick sandy hair and bright blue eyes, and he drawled like a lifelong Texan with a whimsical lack of sub-servience to all authority—especially, it seemed, to Vic Stadter, who was his most frequent boss. Cotton had met Vic at McAllen Airfield, a large aircraft center near the Rio Grande. As he described their first meeting: "I must've stumbled over Vic in a gutter on one of his bad nights."

Vic flew down to see Cotton at his home in Eagle Lake, Texas, as this was no matter to discuss over a telephone.

Cotton wanted nothing to do with it. "It won't work," he told Vic.

Cotton said he had seen enough prisons to know about guards and towers and machine guns and secur-ity. "They'll blow the damn chopper right out of the air!" But Vic was desperate. He stayed for five days, re-peatedly telling Cotton how this prison was a Mexican prison and anyone could bust out, that nobody cared about security, that the weapons were never loaded, that they weren't real guns anyway, just toys, that the guards were totally blind. . . .

Cotton laughed and finally said: "Okay, how much do I get?"

First Cotton had to learn to fly a chopper, and he had to learn it quickly.

Fortunately, Vic had met the man who could teach him, a young helicopter pilot who worked at the Brackett Air Service in Los Angeles where Vic himself had been taking lessons. His name was Roger Guy Hershner. Twenty-nine, bearded, a recent Vietnam War veteran, Hershner had a passion for flying choppers that could best be described as equal to Joel's passion for freedom. Vic immediately hired him away from the school.

Roger was, indeed, a diligent teacher, grateful for payment for what he loved to do. If it was all very strange to him, this super-special assignment, he was discreet enough not to ask any questions. He was enjoying himself too much to bother. Hershner had always been that sort of kid, the type to live and let live, and he found his pleasures along the way. He was born into the conservative traditions of Mansfield, Ohio. His father was a carpenter, his mother a beautician, two solid people who enjoyed their work and each other. He grew up there, graduating high school with no outstanding credentials. He played pretty fair piano and a not-so-fair trombone, but he loved music and it showed. He was a good swimmer and took summer jobs as a life guard, and then he bummed around for a while. Shortly after the family moved to Glendora, California, Roger went into the service. He served as a ground crew technician working on helicopters in Vietnam, and for the first time in his life became fascinated by flying. When he got out, he made use of the GI Bill and studied flying, staying with his first love, the helicopter. He had barely five hundred hours in the air as a pilot when he got a job as an instructor at the Brackett Air Service. He enjoyed that, too. He flew a lot and he met a lot of interesting people. Every once in a while, he met some fascinating ones—like Victor E. Stadter and the man he called "Cotton."

Getting a pilot was only one of Vic's problems. He also needed the dimensions of the prison courtyard where the chopper would land and the height of the wall over which it would fly. Hoping to save time and money, Vic sent a small Minox camera down to Pussy with instructions for Joel to photograph the patio from all angles. Not a simple job, he realized, since it would have to be done furtively. Vic had debated this idea, balancing the obvious dangers of detection with the advantages of involving Joel in this way, psychological advantages, as it were. He could also assume that Joel would be cautious, for all his eagerness, for such was his nature. If it became too risky to take photographs, Joel would hold off.

"The camera delighted me. As soon as I got it, I wanted to go out to the yard and shoot, but it was twilight and there would have been no point to it. I waited until morning, as impatient as a kid with a new toy. I'd always liked photography, and felt certain I could handle this type of job on the first go-round. I played around with the camera in my cell, practicing secret sighting. Castro kept teasing me, asking 'What're you taking pictures for?' 'Pictures? What pictures?' I replied.

"The next day, I took the precaution of rubbing wet dirt over the shining metal in hopes of helping to conceal it. As cautiously as I could, I did what I'd been instructed to do, moving from one side of the yard to the other, even setting Castro against the wall so that Vic might get a fairly accurate estimate of its height.

"One of the prisoners did ask me what I had with me, and I told him it was a tape recorder. He said 'oh.' "

Cotton was disappointed with the pictures. They came out well enough, but the dimensions were too obscure to be accurately determined. He insisted on getting someone in to pace them off, suggesting that Joel himself do it. But prisoners in the ordinary course of events do not go around measuring the prison without arousing considerable curiosity.

Unfortunately, Pussy was off in the hills between Mexico City and Brownsville, Texas, stashing five-gallon fuel cans for the helicopter's getaway, and could not be reached.

"Why don't you do it Vic?" suggested Cotton, knowing full well that Vic would never set foot inside that Mexican prison again, certainly not under such suspicious circumstances.

"Hell, why don't *you* tell the warden you plan on bringing a chopper in there and *ask* him for the dimensions?"

"You can't kid me," Cotton went on. "It ain't that you're scared of getting caught, it's just that you can pace it all right, but you can't count high enough."

As was customary, Vic called on a relative to do the job.

Eugene Wilmoth is an impressive 6'2" salesman for a commercial soap manufacturing company, a well-dressed, well-spoken man with a distinguished air. He is also Vic Stadter's brother-in-law. Vic knew that Mexican bureaucrats would be impressed by such a man. Wilmoth went to Mexico City where Vic's friends were instructed to get him into Santa Marta as an "official"—any kind of official would do.

Vic's Mexico City confederates were bothered by the awesome fact that the very distinguished and well-spoken American could not speak a word of Spanish. To say the least, this limited his capacities as an investigatory official. The solution was the most bold-faced one imaginable: the devil take the language barrier—Big Gene would be brought into Santa Marta as a taciturn member of the Venezuelan consulate, a specialist in penology who had heard glowing tributes paid to the Acatitla Prison and requested permission to be escorted through it.

And it happened that when tall, silent Eugene Wilmoth entered those austere grounds, he was treated as an important visiting dignitary; nothing was withheld from his surveillance. The warden himself headed the hour-long tour, inundating this towering VIP with a barrage of descriptions to which the Venezuelan penologist nodded in agreement and occasionally even deigned to extend a smile. And when he came to the patio that serviced the prisoners of Dormitory Number One, who was to notice that he stopped for a rather conspicuous moment to take note of certain landmarks —the basketball court, for one, the height of the dormitory wall for another—and who even noticed that for the first time on his tour he paced the entire length and width of the area with one of the prisoners alongside, that annoying little American who had murdered his partner.

Cotton was pleased with the dimensions: the basketball court at the east end would be a problem, but not an insurmountable one under average wind conditions. Still, as he pointed out to Vic, if a strong easterly gust should hit them, there was a danger that the chopper might be driven into the backboard. Given the relationship between the two men, Vic's reply was not surprising: "If so, you'll get a foul shot."

The way Vic read it, a $30,000 Bell model 47 would do the job handily, a small four-seater popular with oil exploration companies operating in the back country. There would be enough power to pull up the plane plus the pilot and prisoner even given Santa Marta's high altitude, especially if they were to strip the chopper of all unnecessary weight—extra seats, doors, trimming, useless gadgets. "You may even have to shave," Vic said to Cotton. "And you could lose some of that fat gut, too."

"Bullshit," Cotton replied. "You got more between your ears than I got anywhere."

"Dammit, Cotton, if you were a woman, I'd say you were carrying triplets."

"Well, they sure as hell wouldn't be yours!"

178

First insult, then slander. They had been at it for years, fully aware of the adolescence of their banter, enjoying these little digs at each other, a comforting way of touching.

"Jesus," said Vic, "the thought alone is sickening."

26 Vic was aware of the clause in the documents associated with Joel Kaplan's inheritance dictating the limitations on his eligibility: Joel could not get his money until such time as he had "become freely established as an actual resident of one of the States of the United States of America." But he was also aware of the civilized Mexican law that defines a jailbreak as legal if no law is broken in the process: in short, if there is no violence to person or property, no bribery of prison officials.

Joel, the eventual beneficiary of Stadter's care in this matter, had been the last to be concerned about such details; so desperate was he for his freedom that he cared little about his fortune. He wanted *out*. Period. He would leave the legal problems that resulted to the lawyers.

It was, therefore, up to Vic, the professional smuggler, to keep the plans within bounds as clearly defined by law and circumscribed by the clause in the trust.

There was first the matter of getting his equipment down to Mexico City. To pass through Customs without incident—especially to pass through with a helicopter —then return with his super-contraband passenger, was no simple matter. Vic needed a cover to justify the entire operation. Having been through such problems before, he had a ready plan: they would travel for a mining company. He would become a mine owner with interests in Central America. In Honduras, say. Everyone knew how valuable a helicopter was to the proper exploitation of a mine, especially when there were difficulties in bringing in supplies.

And so the Milandra Mining Company was born, named after Vic's wife, née Mary Milandra.

"You now own a mining company in Honduras," Vic told Mary over dinner one night.

"Mining what?" she asked.

"Whatever you like. Gold, silver, copper. You name it."

"Diamonds," she quipped.

"In Honduras?" he chided her.

He was feeling good. He liked to operate this way, treading that marvelously delicate line between the legitimate and the fraudulent, yet covering himself so artfully that all those idiot bureaucrats would see nothing. And he liked it especially when everything began to move just the way it was supposed to—like a baseball pitcher working on a no-hit game.

"You're wanted on the phone, dear." Mary called. "It's Irma."

Mary Milandra Stadter was a tower of strength. She had been through thirty years of her husband's derring-do with a record of loyalty and support that would make Vic the envy of any man. She was a small woman who seemed half his size, yet she could face up to him with her own brand of courage and, if necessary, as some of their friends enjoy pointing out, "bring him down to size." She would persevere through the nervous weeks of his adventures as serenely as though he were a successful traveling salesman attending some distant convention. Dutifully, he would phone her, nightly when possible, to let her know how things were going, taking whatever new wrinkles she had to relay, always in that special language they had devised to cover any possible mechanical intrusion on their privacy. Indeed, she had learned to live with his picaresque comings and goings, sensing the rise and fall of his prospects by the sound of his entrance at the kitchen door. He is always amazed at her perceptiveness. "By God, that woman knows me better than I know myself."

It was of special significance, then, that Mary Milandra Stadter should pull up short when she heard Vic's response to what Joel's wife was saying on the phone. His roar of dismay reverberated through their huge old house with such fury that the vase of flowers fell right through her hands.

The no-hitter was shattered: Joel Kaplan had decided that his cellmate of these last three years, Carlos Antonio Contreras Castro, was to be flown out with him.

Let Vic describe his response in his own words: "I told Irma three times, "goddamit, No, *No*, NO! The chopper will never be able to lift another passenger. It will hardly lift two at that altitude. Doesn't he know about thin air?' Besides, I hated what I knew about that talkative sonovabitch. He was the last guy I wanted to take out. He had only a year more to serve. It didn't make a damn bit of sense!"

Joel, however, was adamant. With hindsight, he can picture the validity of Vic's objections. At the time, however, he was not inclined to be reasonable. He did not even know whose idea it was, but he thought it was right that Castro should be included. They had been through so much together, a combined escape seemed logical. Joel could not envision the possible risks. He had neither the detailed information nor the proper vantage point to see into that aeronautic maze. That was Vic's job. Vic was going to get paid for taking him out.

Well, okay. Now he was going to get paid more for taking Castro out, too. From where Joel sat, what was so damned horrendous about that?

Joel tells Irma, Irma calls Vic, Vic calls Judy, Judy calls Choulos, Choulos says: "I don't want to know anything about such matters!" Cotton is practicing with the chopper for two while Joel insists on a lift-off for three. Vic rages at this cruel imposition on his plans and contemplates a refusal to move ahead. Indeed, he now so threatens. He calls Irma, Irma tells Joel, but Joel remains adamant.

And so it would be.

Vic took time to reconsider. When his first full stream of anger drained off, he could admit to himself that his resistance was at least as personal as it was technical. He had allowed his dislikes to intrude on his professionalism. And as professional as he was, this too was typical of him. He worked for money but in a job such as this, he was the kind of man who had to care about the purpose. The spirit had to move him as well as the money. Vic began to see Joel in a different light, defiant instead of meekly submissive, a determined man who was unswervingly loyal. That Vic did not endorse the object of his loyalty was totally irrelevant. Vic understood that. This wasn't supposed to be Vic's ball-game; it was Joel's.

So it was that he began calling Joel "Dan," a code name he used whenever he referred to him. Dan, the steel-driving man, Vic sang.

In the end, Vic was impressed by Joel's charge. He would say later: "That Dan, he's too nice, I guess. It makes him an easy mark. If Jesus Christ were busting out of jail, I'd bet he'd never do what this little guy did."

When Cotton heard the news, he reacted with another baseball term: "Game called on account of rain." The sun would not reappear for Cotton until Vic got himself a new chopper with a turbo supercharger that would give the engine the same power up to 10,000 feet as at sea level. Nor was the problem simplified by the need for a craft no larger than the Bell 47 they had planned to use. He made that clear to Vic. Knowing the dimensions of their target, they had to stay with a small model. "You can't park a Caddie in a VW garage," Cotton stated flat out.

Time was again the enemy. Vic and Cotton spent precious weeks scouring the broad spaces of the Far West, calling or visiting dealers, tracking down all possibilities, until finally, there it was—the most beautiful model of all, courtesy Natrona Services, Casper, Wyoming. Said the ad in the aviation journal: "Bell 47, reconditioned, rebuilt, reupholstered, with new supercharger designed for use in high altitudes, used to fly over 8000 feet." The chopper had been owned by a millionaire, rebuilt for taking friends to a private lake resort high in the Wyoming Rockies, a magnificent plaything with over $100,000 worth of work in it. One could spend a pleasant hour speculating on the likely history of this craft, of the magnificent places it had been to and the elegance of the people it had carried. Now, it would perform for another millionaire in noble duty at the opposite end of the social spectrum.

Vic had visions of buying on credit, a normal down payment and the balance on time. "I had them going pretty good, but the guy checked around and found out who I was. He said: 'Stadter, they say you got a poor life expectancy.' And that meant cash on the barrelhead. Hell, he wouldn't even sell me gas on credit."

Before buying it, Vic insisted on a test flight with a load of four, filling the craft with such big bodies as Doug Wilmoth—the tall seventeen-year-old son of the big "Venezuelan penologist" Gene Wilmoth—weighing at least as much as Joel and Vic, plus Cotton and the pilot. They took off at 5000 feet, not as high as Mexico City, but close enough. "A bit squirrelly," as Vic put it, but they hadn't stripped it yet.

Designed for a maximum weight load of 600 pounds, including gas, it was going to pose a super-squirrelly problem operating at 7200 feet: "I don't like those damn machines. They make no sense at all," said Vic. "You've got to coordinate the rudder, the throttle, the rotary . . . it's a damn mess. They don't have the speed pick-up like a normal airplane. They get tossed around in the least bit of wind. You never know what they're going to do."

He had to pay $65,000 for it.

The pilot agreed to fly Cotton to Denver where they met the helicopter teacher from Glendora, Roger Hershner. There, Hershner and his pupil, Cotton, helicopter-hopped to Houston where Vic was going to put together the operation.

Vic himself was about to leave California, when suddenly his indispensable aide, Pussy, became ill. Pussy complained of a severe headache that had been plaguing him for days. He could cope with the pain, but not the sporadic seizures of blindness. Alarmed, Vic took his friend to a doctor, and, after extensive examination, the diagnosis indicated a brain tumor. Immediate surgery was advised. But Pussy was not a man who would submit to the knife, not while he could still walk. In fact, he had other ideas for therapy, ideas that would take him to an Indian reservation in New Mexico where he had spent some time in the past. Among those people lived an amazing witch doctor who performed miraculous cures with special herbs and ancient incantations. . . .

Joel, meanwhile, was kicking up a fuss, demanding to be informed of their progress. Clearly, Vic's policy of keeping Joel in ignorance was causing problems, especially now that Pussy would not be around to assuage the prisoner's anxieties. Somehow, Joel had to be reassured that the wheels were turning, that all obstacles were being overcome, that it was only a question of time when E-Day would be declared. The trouble was, this had to be done without telling Joel any details to substantiate it. It followed that Vic would dispatch someone who didn't know any; that was to be his new son-in-law, husband to his only daughter, Mary Jane, an extremely attractive young lady in her mid-twenties who herself had served nobly on a number of missions in the past. The son-in-law's instructions were simply to pacify the overanxious prisoner. "No matter what he asks you," Vic advised him, "just keep telling him not to worry." A few days later, the son-in-law reported back that his mission was absolutely impossible, that he left Kaplan "looking sicker than the last dead man I saw." Vic later commented that his son-in-law "wasn't the best pacifier in the world, but he was all I could come up with at the moment."

Houston was a familiar locale for Vic and Cotton, offering first-rate flying facilities and attendant technical benefits, a large enough city to maintain anonymity while they put all the pieces of the operation together.

Vic had fashioned a general plan, allowing himself plenty of room to vary the particulars whenever a situation called for it. This flexibility had always been his habit. Experience had taught him that he could operate more effectively by improvising than by attempting to stick to rigid prearrangements. Too many little things were liable to go wrong, and usually did. He had learned to move only one step at a time, keeping his plan simple and adaptable, avoiding split-second meetings and iron-clad commitments whenever a looser procedure was possible.

186

Having decided to fly Joel back to the States in a fast single-engine Cessna 210, Vic traded in his more cumbersome twin-engine 310, which conceivably would have attracted greater attention at the smaller Mexican airports he intended to use. As with the helicopter, the Cessna was registered in the name of the Milandra Mining Company. Indeed, he had papers prepared for everything, including a birth certificate in the name of Joel David Kaplan—forged by an expert in Los Angeles —which, with that marvelous circuitous logic of a smuggler, "would insure that Joel would re-enter the U.S. legally."

Cotton, however, still had to be convinced that the helicopter escape was possible. To accomplish this, Vic sent him down to Santa Marta a number of times to see for himself. Cotton would fly commercial airlines to Mexico City where Irma Vasquez Calderon Kaplan would meet him with a chauffeur-driven Renault (she hated to drive in city traffic). He'd be taken to Acatitla Prison, which they would drive around while he drew sketches of the exterior layout and the exact locations of the guard towers as they related to the courtyard of Dormitory Number One, where "the hit" would be made. Furtively, he studied the guards through binoculars, taking note of their attitudes and their access to rifles, noting that they did not carry their arms but kept them in a special booth a few feet away. He mapped out the best possible flight route for the chopper to take in and out, figuring everything from the angle of the setting sun (if the guards were going to shoot, make them shoot into a blinding sunset) to the flow of the prevailing winds.

In time, Cotton became convinced of its possibilities. In fact, thoroughly convinced. The way he figured it, he could bring the chopper in and out in less than forty seconds. Unless those guards were forewarned, they'd never have time to get a shot off. With typically supreme confidence, he told Vic it would be "as simple as getting laid in a Mexican whorehouse." To which Vic replied, "You oughta know, you ain't never been laid anyplace else!"

With typical caution, however, Vic was wary of Irma's chauffeur. Who in hell was he anyway? He could easily picture "the enemy" sneaking an operative into such a vital job, a man with big ears and a quick eye. Once, Vic waited for Cotton's return to the Mexico City airport with Irma and then followed the little Renault back to town and Irma's apartment, tailing the chauffeur in a classic imitation of a third-rate private eye—very third rate since, as it turned out, the man never drove over twenty-five miles per hour and was, therefore, practically impossible to tail without detection.

Joel, meanwhile, had been conjuring up an escape with everything in it but the kitchen sink, so violent were his frustrations. His was a plan of old-fashioned ferocity, with a special car parked outside the main gate that would be smoke-bombed by the Cessna 210 as a decoy, the chopper sliding in a few minutes later from the opposite side of the prison with machine guns blazing at the tower guards, flak suits and rifles ready as they made their getaway, and, maybe, as Cotton had kiddingly added, one of those bombs that explode into a mushroom cloud.

Said Vic: "Joel must have seen too many movies. There was no need for any of that, you don't have to work that way. It should always be done quietly; a pro knows that. You don't shoot at the guards, you wave at them."

But to assure Joel, he passed word to him that they had mounted the latest machine gun equipment they could find.

The helicopter continued to dominate their concern. They had attacked the luxuriously endowed million-

188

aire's toy, stripping it of all unnecessary material, rip-
ping out the plush upholstery, paneling, secondary
seats, taking off the door—anything of any weight that
could be removed, was removed. If it lost its interior
cosmetic appeal in the process, the supercharged flying
machine could only find its job simpler. But it was the
exterior that Vic began to worry about: what of its very
presence over Mexico City, especially when it would be
approaching Santa Marta and the prison? Wouldn't
people be asking what it was doing there? Vic began
to wonder whether there was anything he could do to
the helicopter's appearance that would justify its awesome presence.

The best he could come up with was a blatantly
obvious ploy, the painting of the word *Policia* on a huge
canvas that would be secured to the chopper with a
rope run through grommets, to be mounted during the
last lap of the rescue itself. He went to a surplus store
and found an adaptable canvas, and, late at night,
painted the big black letters himself. He then faced
the problem of how to bring such a provocative sign into
Mexico; its discovery would only create disastrously
suspicious reactions—especially if it were found hidden
inside the chopper. Vic was planning to drive to Mexico
City, and he considered burying the canvas in the trunk
of his car—but then, what if something else went awry
and officials chose to shake down the car?

In the end, Vic gave up and discarded the whole
idea, fearing that the possible gain of such a sign was
not worth the risk of its discovery.

The episode irritated him for he had spent too much
time on a worthless action. To compound it, he had
carelessly junked the canvas in a large empty fifty-five
gallon oil drum, realizing only later, while having
lunch at the airport coffee shop, how stupid that was,
and he hurried back to retrieve it "before some nosy
bastard might discover it and ask questions." He fished
it out and was taking it to his car when he found him-

self face to face with the pretty little Guatemalan lady named Irma.

He was surprised and not surprised. He had talked with her several times during the frantic activities of recent days and he'd caught some of her husband's wails of desperation. Now, here she was, having flown all the way to Houston with a brand new Polaroid camera in her large woolen bag, her bright brown eyes twinkling with Joel's demand that she get a picture of that helicopter with herself standing alongside, thereby assuring him of its authenticity. Vic graciously consented to take the picture, and, since the stripped Bell 47 was up in the air at the moment, he did not think it impolitic to select another chopper that happened to be handy, a much more glamorous model. The picture was immediately developed to Irma's satisfaction and Vic's quiet amusement.

It was not a wasted meeting, however. Irma allowed that she had always wanted to fly in such a craft, having seen the Attorney General's helicopter fly over Mexico City many times. Vic was too tightly tuned in to miss the significance of Irma's remark, and he pounced on it.

"How do you know it's the Attorney General's?" he demanded.

"It's all blue," she replied.

Well, that was that, Vic thought. All the damn thing needed was a paint job.

"When Irma brought me the photograph, I was too sick to care. I'd sent her to get it because I'd lost all trust in this mess. I was going through a really bad time and I just couldn't cope with myself. I would think one day, I'll never get out of here, and the next thing I'd be screaming, get me out, get me out! Yes, unreasonable of me, I knew, but I'd lost the ability to sit there while others controlled my fate. I had to know what was happening and Vic, the old crab, had refused to tell. While I could understand the need for security, I didn't see why it had to include me. I got to hate him for that. Weeks would go by and I would hear nothing. Irma would call him and he'd feed her a lot of silly platitudes about how everything was moving along fine, but I knew better, I'd heard that too many times in the past. The way I was feeling, I would have bet that the whole plan was turning into a terrible farce and they would blame it on my insisting on taking Castro along.

"Then I began to have my own mixed feelings about that. Why had I done it? Had I ruined everything by antagonizing Stadter? It was obvious he didn't like Castro, to put it mildly. Was I trying to show him that I was the important one?

"I was sick. I was feeling terrible . . . body, mind, spirit—all hurting. I looked at the picture of Irma standing beside the helicopter and I realized how stupid it was, how the man must have laughed at her. It was another indication of how far gone I was, and that depressed me all the more.

"Later that night, I began suffering from a bad stomach cramp. I'd had pretty much of everything since I'd been in prison, but this was something different. I began running a fever, and then I felt a sharp pain on my right side. That bothered me terribly. Trying to fake an appendix attack had taught me the symptoms and now I began to fear a real attack. I knew it was silly, paranoid even, but I couldn't help it. I knew such a thing wasn't possible. I had a bad stomach, that was all. Any other prognosis was the result of my state of mind. I was sick, but it would pass. I began to will it so. After all, I was a man who could will himself sick —so I could will myself well—couldn't I?"

Vic was looking for a woman, a special kind of woman, a woman who looked like a high-class whore. He needed her to create the proper setting for his automobile trip into Mexico. From his experience, a man did not drive into Mexico alone, not if he wished to avoid the suspicions of the dozen officials he would confront in the course of his journey. Curiously, a lone man set up a dangerous reaction: a loner must surely be up to some illicit operation.

But a well-dressed man in a big flashy car with a handsome whore with dyed hair tossed up to the roof and an inch and a half of makeup, well, that was easy to understand. He had gotten away with that too often before not to use it again. His beautiful daughter, Mary Jane, knew exactly how to handle the role. He had trained her, using her on various operations in the past; she knew just what to say, how to look, how to act at all times. So he called Mary Jane, telling her to pack her bag and get hold of her big blond wig. He needed her for a week in Mexico for the Dan job.

For the first time, she said no. Her husband did not want her to be doing that sort of thing any more. He didn't like the image of his wife putting on such an act, nor even associating in that sort of adventure.

It drove Vic raging mad. He had not only lost his A-Number-One decoy, he was now forced to face the always complex problem of finding a new one. The way he saw it, it was just as difficult to find the right woman as it had been to find the right chopper pilot. "You need a woman who can keep her mouth shut, and there ain't too many of them!"

He went through his list, finding no candidate. Then he remembered a big blonde he had seen a number of times at a truck-stop diner back near his home in Glendora, a beefy Italian woman who wore her blonde wig "up to the roof" and painted herself up to make less of the estimated thirty-five years and 75,000 miles she had on her history.

"She looked like a perfect whore so I made her an offer. Naturally, she accepted."

He needed a proper car to complete the image.

Preferably, a Cadillac—a large Coupe de Ville colored in Baroque Bronze, as the dealers describe it, a car that symbolized a touristy showboat built for a pleasure weekend, a reliable car that could move when it had to, a car exactly like the Caddie owned by the operative named Cotton, né Harvey Orville Dail.

"Okay," said Cotton, "but how much?"

"Well, you can have the blonde."

"Shee-it, I ought to charge *you* for servicing her."

So it was that Vic was finally ready to proceed south.

And then Irma reached him at his hotel with the latest catastrophe in the continuing saga of her husband's quest for freedom: Joel's appendix was seriously inflamed.

Vic winced. The prospects of a week's delay, at a minimum, might easily destroy the entire plan. He so hated the thought, he wanted to believe Joel's protestation that all Mexican doctors were capable of being wrong 100 per cent of the time. Indeed, Joel wanted to go, insisting on ignoring the pain in his side. But Vic refused to take such a risk with a man's health. To ease Joel's mind, he told him that he was not prepared to leave for a week, anyway. And that was that.

The God of the Appendix was apparently no fan of Joel's. One thing seemed absolutely certain: there could be no escape while that useless organ remained inside him. Joel went under the knife, successfully, and as it turned out, fortunately. As the surgeon told Irma: "If he hadn't submitted to surgery, he would probably have died by the following morning."

Said Joel: "I was learning to hate that hospital."

27

The target date was set back ten days—just enough time for Joel's stitches to begin to itch.

Joel sent impatient word that he was ready.

"Then," as Vic recalls, "the shit hit the fan."

Cotton sat down next to Vic in the Houston airport coffee shop with a toothpick in his mouth even before he had eaten a bite. It was not a good sign.

"Vic," he said, "I ain't ready to fly that thing."

"What!"

"I need more time. I don't trust those choppers yet. Give me another week."

"No more delays!"

"A few days practice before we go. . . ."

"You've got seven or eight more hours practice just flying the damn thing down to Mexico. Work on it then."

Pause.

"Vic, it's no good."

"Dammit, Cotton, you got shit in your neck?"

"Vic, you know I don't rat out. I just don't think I can handle it yet."

Vic felt the bubble rising inside him. It was unbelievable. By God, it just might really be that that poor sonovabitch in Mexico was jinxed right up to his ass. It just might be that there was no way anyone could get him out.

194

He looked at Cotton and, for one terrible moment, it crossed his mind that maybe, just maybe, "they" had gotten to him. The moment passed.

"Dammit, Cotton, I always knew you were an old lady."

"Shee-it. If I was, you would've raped me a dozen years ago."

"It's lucky you got that Caddie. Otherwise, I'd send you back to the old lady's home."

Of one thing, Vic was certain: there would be no further delay. If he had to talk the blonde into flying the chopper, he was heading south immediately. Neither he nor Joel could afford to waste another day. Especially Joel, who was literally itching to go. Vic sensed that the man had really been disintegrating over the eight or nine months since he had met him. "If we waited another week, I'd be taking out a basket case."

Besides, he did not want to hang around Houston any longer, not with that bright blue helicopter, the green and white Cessna, the big blonde whore, the Baroque Bronze Cadillac. It was the same old problem: the stall. "You just can't afford to let your face be seen day after day, people start asking questions, an official starts nosing around. Hell, with my rep, the whole of U.S. Customs and Immigration would be pushing their grubby pencils in my face. And there we were, sitting in Texas with all our guts showing, and Cotton wanted more time."

Vic said "No" to Cotton. Then he said a lot more to the instructor, the bearded young man named Roger Guy Hershner.

"Roger, we ought to have a little chat, you and me."

"I've got to check the landing gear, Vic."

"Sit down, Roger. I've got a proposition for you."

"Oh?"

"The way I see it, you don't know what this whole thing is about. Right?"

"None of my business, I guess."

"Right. Well, we're involved in something, it's not entirely on the square, it's legal in the U.S.A. but not in Mexico. You see, we're gonna be stealing some test ore down there, it's at a mine in Honduras, we're gonna go in with the chopper and take it out."

"Oh."

"It's a dangerous business, Roger. I gotta admit there are Indians down there, and maybe they'll shoot at you, but they don't shoot too good, I guarantee you . . ."

"What!"

"Look, I'll pay you some real good money."

"You mean, you want me to fly the chopper all the way down to Honduras and take out that ore."

"Well, yeah."

"Well . . . sure, Vic. Why not."

When in trouble improvise. This was Vic's way. There was no way to plan an operation worth a damn, there was always something going wrong. You had to rely on your instincts and your luck.

Sometimes, you needed a lot of luck.

Papers, equipment, personnel. Three machines and four bodies. Together, then separately, they began the great trek south to the border on a mission of mercy and money, flying the pennants of the Milandra Mining Company, their valiant commander dressed up in shiny Texas boots and striped bell-bottom trousers, his flaring mustache perfectly trimmed, sitting tall in the seat behind the wheel of Cotton's shimmering bronze Caddie, with his fair lady at his side. And Cotton, having been relieved of his chopper-charge by mutual consent, now returned to flying legitimate aircraft, the Cessna 210, which he was to pilot to the border city of Brownsville, check in with appropriate papers, then go on to fly the firm's plane to Honduras; all strictly legitimate.

Before they left, however, there was one final bit of

tampering to be done. The Cessna's registration, clearly marked on its fuselage, read 9462X before Cotton attacked it with a wad of tape. A few artfully placed strips made it read 8482X. When Cotton took off for the border, he radioed in his correct registration, 9462X, to U.S. authorities. But when he landed at the Mexican border town of Matamoros, the plane was registered the way it read—8482X.

There were no limits to the benefits that might be derived from confusing the Mexicans.

Cotton then flew on to Tampico, Mexico, where he checked into the Hotel Impala to wait for further contact from his boss.

Meanwhile, Roger Hershner climbed aboard his own true love, the supercharged Bell Model 47, and flew it to McAllen Airfield, adjacent to the Mexican border; there, he was joined by Vic and the blonde and, incidentally, twelve empty five-gallon fuel cans, to be transferred to the chopper for use on the return trip. All of Pussy's stashes had been stolen by Indians.

For Vic, the first test of his foresight and fortune was faced at the offices of Mexican Immigration at the border town of Reinosa. The flashy Cadillac and its showy passengers passed with flying colors. As Vic explained it: "I told them I was just an old tourist going down for a few days of fun and frolic. Sure, I was married, but this was not my wife, just a friend who needed some company. By Jesus, I even winked at them. They took one good look at the blonde—I don't know why, but they love those blondes—and I knew they weren't going to remember me, just her. I slipped them a ten spot and they gave us a tourist card, then off we went through what they call the 'free zone' and on to the Mexican Customs. It's pretty much the same there. They're supposed to be looking for contraband but they're really looking for a payoff. I gave them another ten spot and they smiled like true gentlemen, put stickers on the suitcases (without opening them) and we became bona fide tourists. It's all very predictable if you play your cards right. They're poor guys, they're good people, this is the way they make their living; you're supposed to know that and play the game, you pay the ten spot and everybody is happy, because if you don't they'll give you a bad time one way or another and I needed that like I needed this blonde for a wife."

It was not as simple for Roger and the chopper. Vic drove to the airport at Reinosa, just to be sure Roger was not in trouble—only to find that he was. Again, predictably, while a married Texan with his concubine were sacrosanct, a helicopter on business, however clean, was fair game.

Vic found Roger trapped inside the office, getting worked on by a batch of Customs people, all of them jabbering away at the harrassed American who could speak no Spanish. Helpless to intercede at this point, Vic and the blonde sat at the restaurant counter over a cup of coffee and watched the action through the glass door, unable to hear any of it.

Then, finally, they let him go.

Roger came out smiling, like a fighter who'd just won a tough bout.

"Welcome to Mexico, kid," Vic said.

"Is it any easier going back?"

"Only on Christmas Eve."

"Wow."

"You look worried," put in the blonde.

"If they lock me up, Vic, can you get me out?"

Vic had to laugh out loud. "Why, sure, Roger. Easy as pie."

Roger's helicopter flight plan read that he was to proceed to La Pesca, a small fishing village about a hundred miles south of Reinosa. Roger could fill up on gas there, as the airfield was small and had no radio. This was Vic's way of maintaining silence with the authorities, all part of his over-all precautionary plan to avoid any possible confrontations. At Reinosa, they filled the twelve gas cans, reloaded them into the chopper, and the two machines took off, one by land, the other by air. To Vic's great delight, he went barreling down the open road fast enough to keep the chopper always in view, the ultimate insult to all aircraft. He was thinking of a thousand future barroom arguments as he fancied himself waiting for the helicopter at the meeting spot of Tamuin, the tortoise beating the hare— Vic was laughing so hard that he did not immediately hear the right front tire blow. The car swerved violently off the road, ran treacherously close to a deep ditch by the road bed, skittering and screeching until he was finally able to contain it.

"Very funny," said the blonde.

Vic changed tires, thinking all the while how close he had come to ruining the entire expedition, ignoring possible injuries, considering only the rupture of schedules. If the car had veered a few feet more, they'd be in that ditch, and then what?

It was small satisfaction, then, that he caught up with the chopper less than thirty minutes later.

Roger was having his own troubles. He arrived at the La Pesca airfield only to discover that not only was there no radio, there was also no gas. It was just as Vic had warned him: never expect what you're told to expect. The question was, where was he supposed to go to get more fuel? Time was beginning to press on him, for he had to do his flying in daylight only. He knew Vic was going through Ciudad Victoria, that, whenever possible, Vic wanted to avoid having the helicopter in the same town with him. But Roger, left with no choice, flew to Victoria to refuel. His assignment was to take those twelve full five-gallon gas cans and make a number of stashes to cover his return to the States. He had wondered about that. A helicopter runs through fifteen gallons an hour, averages 65 miles per hour. The twelve cans would total sixty gallons, enough for four hours flying or a little more than 250 miles. The shortest route to Honduras was a lot longer than that, requiring any number of stops at airports for refueling. This business of stashing away five-gallon cans in hidden fields did not make much sense to him. But then, he wasn't getting paid to think. It was like the army, maybe even including getting shot at. The big difference this time around was the flying, to say nothing of the money. He would be making more in one week than he could save in a year. Then, too, there was Mexico. As Vic had told him, a man could have a good time in Mexico.

But first he had to stash those gas cans. He flew south from Victoria and found "a real tight hole in the jungle" a few miles west of the tiny village of Ajascador, at least a mile from the nearest trail. He found a clearing and, hovering over it, marked the exact location on his map, then dropped to the ground and unloaded.

Next stop, the city of Tamuin, for his first night in Mexico.

Vic, arriving in Tamuin, immediately telephoned Cotton in Tampico. Both man and machine had arrived in fine shape. Vic reported the same at his end. They would proceed according to the prearranged plan. Cotton indicated he was glad to hear that, looked forward to their next meeting, then hung up after the usual pleasantries of two men involved in a routine business matter.

Tamuin is a quiet town, a few miles off route 85 to Mexico City, not listed in any of the tourist guides. The hotel is even quieter; situated outside the town itself, it is an old inn surrounded by heavy foliage, with old

Spanish decor, arched ceilings, and tile floors. To this hidden spot, Vic brought Roger and the blonde.

It was the kind of place he loved, where every courtesy was returned with courtesy, where the place itself was real and ageless and free of imitations and all the garish nonsense designed to impress people. They spent the evening leisurely sitting through a simple but excellent Mexican dinner. No radio. No TV. They had moved from the slick world of the neon motels to a setting from an earlier century.

A perfect place for this trio, for Vic had decided that, on the following day, they would make "the hit" at Acatitla.

28

In Tampico, on the morning of Wednesday, August 18, 1971, Cotton rose early, had a quick cup of coffee, and taxied to the airport. The Cessna was parked safely, as he had left it. He would leave it again, this time taking a commercial airline flight to Mexico City. Vic did not want the Cessna coming and going unnecessarily.

At 9:30, Cotton arrived at Mexico City's International Airport. He walked over to the airport Holiday Inn and waited for Irma, whom he had contacted the previous day. She picked him up a few minutes before ten and they drove out to Santa Marta for what appeared to be a routine visit to the prisoner, Joel Kaplan.

Joel waited for them in one of the cold basement rooms used for conjugal visits. "I thought there'd be less chance of our being overheard. Besides, it was nicer to be with Irma down there. You don't have to talk through wire-mesh as you do upstairs.

"Irma came with Cotton. She was worried about how I was feeling after the operation and all. I told her I was all right. She wanted to know what I'd done all morning. Sometimes, I made up a fantasy about how I'd gone sailing on my yacht, or gone for a canter in the woods—it was a little game we played. But this time, I don't quite know why, I told it to her just as it had happened: I'd gotten up at 6:30, the usual hour, reported to roll call, went back to bed. Got up again at 9:00, washed up, had coffee, read the newspaper, took a stroll in the yard. . . . It was one of those times together when you sort of muddle through a conversation just for the sake of saying something. She nodded and said she'd see me tomorrow as usual, and then Cotton came over.

"He didn't stay long, just long enough to give me the instructions. He said they were ready to come for us, but he wasn't sure exactly when. Castro and I were to start walking the courtyard that evening at exactly 6:30, and to stay out there until 7. If they didn't come for us that evening, we were to come back again the next evening and do the same. And again the next. Always from 6:30 to 7. For identification, we were each to carry a newspaper. That was all. Just a newspaper. The helicopter would touch ground and remain there for no more than ten seconds. We had ten seconds to get aboard. That was all there was to it. There would be no further communications.

"I saw Castro back in the cell and I told him the instructions, and he said, 'Sure, sure.' I didn't want to talk to him about it so I went to my bed to take my nap. He always respected my nap, I guess, because he knew I'd been so ill. Besides, there was nothing special to talk about. I suppose he was thinking about this new girl friend of his, Maribel, anticipating her arrival. Aside from that, we both believed that absolutely nothing was going to happen."

It was shortly after noon when Irma dropped Cotton back at the airport for his return flight to Tampico. Cotton spoke Spanish poorly, but he made certain that Irma knew how important it was that she get out of town that day. She had her instructions: she was to fly to Los Angeles and, once there, call Mary Stadter, who would take care of her. The baby would be left with her mother in Mexico until things cooled off.

Cotton stood by the car and said good-bye to her, trying to indicate that he would not be seeing her again. To cement this, he chose to cross the language barrier the only way he knew: he drew her to him and affectionately kissed her cheek.

Boarding the plane for Tampico, Cotton wondered if he had convinced Irma that this really was it.

Vic and the blonde drove to the Pachuca airport where Roger was waiting, right on schedule. And right on *their* schedule, Mexican officials were hammering away at him. The questions were predictable despite the fact all the answers were in his flight plan. Question: What was he doing in Pachuca in a helicopter? Answer: Traveling south for the Milandra Mining Company. Question: Yes, that's what is written on the flight plan. But what are you *really* doing in Pachuca?

The trouble was complicated by the presence of one Captain Carlos Franco, an important Mexican air official who was the inspiration behind the fuss these underlings were kicking up. Vic, knowing the Mexican mentality at moments when the bureaucracy is at work, sized up the situation instantly: "They're born to suspicion when a gringo shows up because they can always smell out a possible deal. They look at you like you were the biggest thief since Cortez and they shake their heads no matter what you tell them. 'No, sorry, it can't be true, you gotta be lying, maybe we oughta throw you in the brig for a night or two.' They can do it, too, especially when there's a VIP standing by.

"They didn't like the helicopter. I guess they don't see too many of them. They figured it had to be up to no good, and Captain Franco, thinking, well, here's a chance to make some sort of big investigation—oh, they're hot shit with the investigations, they can investigate the balls off a brass monkey. And that was all I needed, a day in some crummy Mexican office while the calls went out to every government agency they could think of calling, and God knows what they'd come up with."

There was no question but that Vic was worried. He seemed so worried that Roger was amazed at the sight of him, the sudden pale intensity, the tremulous tone of voice. Roger never suspected that Vic could ever be vulnerable. But Vic was unendingly resourceful. What Roger saw and did not understand was the creation of a new character, a big, dumb Texan who was too stupid to offer a bribe.

"I knew that if I tried to bribe him, he'd immediately suspect that something was really wrong," Vic recalled. So he played his role to the hilt: all he wanted was to get his equipment through to the south and have a little fun in Mexico City along the way. Again, the wink to indicate the blonde.

"It was the blonde who made it all seem legit. The VIP took one last look at her, a long look, and bless her soul, she gave him a smile and puckered her lips just enough to straighten him up. Then he smiled for the first time since we'd arrived. Okay, he said. Go ahead.

"I could've kissed her then, but that *really* would have been stupid."

The Captain left with his lackeys and the supervision of the Pachuca airfield was returned to the man who did the work, the kind of little man whom Vic always appreciated: "a poor, simple guy trying to make a living without necessarily swindling someone." He walked over to him with a tired smile, handed him 20 pesos, and asked him to watch the helicopter while they went to town for a little food.

Vic had another job to perform: it was time to have a heart-to-heart talk with Roger.

At the restaurant he sent the blonde to powder her nose and sat Roger in a quiet booth.

"Roger, there's a little matter we got to talk over."

"That mine?"

"Well, yeah."

"It's not in Honduras, is it."

"Well, no, it ain't."

"I figured."

"Roger, as a matter of fact, it ain't even a mine."

"Oh?"

"It's a prison."

Pause.

"A what?"

"Well, now, listen carefully, Roger. We're down here on a rescue operation. I know it sounds pretty heavy, but I do it all the time. There's danger to it, and I want you to think it over before you say anything. You have the right to back out and you'll be paid no matter what. But it's all set up, so we don't anticipate any trouble. It's going to be safe enough. You really don't have much to worry about."

"I'm supposed to fly the chopper into *a prison*?"

"Yeah. There'll be two guys waiting for you."

"*Two* guys?"

"Yeah. One's my friend and the other's his friend. Think it over. There'll be a nice bonus for you when it's done."

They had their coffee and nothing was said. Then Vic checked in to register the flight plan. They were back at the airport, as Vic noted later, in sight of the chopper, before Roger opened up.

"Okay, Vic. I'll do it."

"Fine, Roger."

"Just one question. Okay?"

"Sure."

"What's this guy in for? Your friend."

Vic thought, well, he might as well give it to him straight.

206

"Murder," he said.

Roger shook his head and almost smiled. "Just like Vietnam," he mumbled.

It would be useless to ask Vic what he would have done if Roger had refused. He simply would not be able to reply. That is Vic's way. His mind can face an issue when it has to, spurred by the juices that necessity places upon him. If Roger had turned him down? Well, Vic would say, "I don't rightly know." Perhaps he would have talked Cotton back into flying the chopper. Perhaps he would have flown it in himself. Perhaps he would've trained the blonde. . . .

But Vic was already concentrating on the next problem, the treacherous matter of aerodynamics that had worried him all along: could the helicopter actually fly the escape pattern in this altitude? The answer, then, was to test it in perfectly simulated conditions. He would fly it "over the prison wall"—in this instance, the adjacent hangar, somewhat higher than the real wall and about the same width as the entire courtyard. Excellent test, he thought, especially since they were at 7400 feet, 200 feet higher than Santa Marta, and the three of them aboard would be heavier than the two prisoners.

"Oh, no," said the blonde. "I'm not flying in that crate."

"Get in!" snapped Vic.

"Is it safe?" she protested.

"No. Get in!"

Roger revved up the engine 200 rpm over Red Line, then threw in the clutch, and up it went like a balloon filled with helium when a child lets go of the string. Roger took it over the hangar easily, then brought it back for a perfect pinpoint landing.

"Okay," said Vic. "Now let's try it again."

"This is fun," said the blonde.

"Make her pay fare," said Roger.

"Shut up and fly," said Vic.

They all laughed, fears drowned out by success. Victory makes lovers of us all, Vic thought. Victor the victor—at least for the moment. He wondered what the rest of the day would be like.

They left the chopper at Pachuca and drove the twenty kilometers to the village of Actopan where, if all went well, they would meet Cotton with the Cessna. As they drove by the village, Vic had to laugh, for there was Cotton, strolling along the road from the landing strip, barely two blocks from the local restaurant. He had just landed the 210, maybe three minutes before.

Actopan was a small friendly village of 8,515 people, mostly Indians of Otomi heritage. The village spread out over a sprawling hilly area some 6500 feet high. Wednesday was market day, and the town was bustling.

The landing strip was nothing more than part of a cow pasture, an emergency area for planes in trouble. Vic had used it on other occasions, though not for emergencies. If it lacked facilities, it had more than enough privacy, which was exactly why he was there: he'd never seen anyone in the neighborhood except an occasional cow.

On this day, however, Vic brought in enough action to scare away all the cows in the neighborhood.

United for the first time since Houston, the team moved quickly. Vic put Roger in the 210 for Cotton to show him the exact route to Santa Marta—or, as Vic put it, "fly him over the mine and be absolutely sure to show him the right hole to drop into!"

There were a few predictable erotic jokes triggered by that remark, and though they amused Cotton, Roger was too tense to enjoy them, and Vic too busy. He took the blonde to the Actopan marketplace and there he bought Joel some work clothes. Pants, shirt, jacket. He had all the right sizes in his notes. He also bought a few sandwiches and fruit juices for Roger, a blanket, and, just for luck, a fifth of Scotch, Old Smuggler, of course. Vic later noted with a boisterous pride in his steady good luck that he was able to find a bottle of his favorite brand stuck away in that remote village marketplace.

He was back at the field just before 5 P.M., a few minutes after Cotton returned from his flight with Roger. Roger was tense, Vic could see, but the trip had gone well. The route to Santa Marta was laid out perfectly for him, plotted on the proper World Aeronautical Chart; he had been shown exactly what roads to follow, and, for a pilot with Hershner's experience, there was really no way he could possibly get lost. He had seen the prison and Cotton had shown him "the exact hole" he was to drop the chopper into. Like an athlete before a big game, he was all primed to go.

"Man, it'll be a breeze!" Roger boasted to Vic.

Sure, Vic thought. If the tower guards don't shoot at you, if Joel and that big-mouth cellmate are actually there waiting, if the stupid flying machine does what he'd paid $65,000 for it to do, if the entire goddamn Mexican air force doesn't follow him back here, if, if, if. . . .

It was crazy, but Vic's biggest worry was Joel. He could picture Joel being late or careless or even indifferent. He could even picture him saying to Castro that there wasn't going to be any escape, certainly not tonight, they wouldn't be coming tonight, it was too soon, and he'd linger in his cell for another ten minutes, or he'd be in the can, or something.

"Cotton," he said, "are you sure you told him to be out there at 6:30 starting tonight?"

"Tonight? Hell, no. I think I said something about hitting there next Tuesday around midnight. Didn't you want the whole thing to be covered by darkness next week?"

"Very funny," Vic replied.

"They'll be there," Cotton said.

Vic nodded. He sensed he had covered everything. There was simply no point in waiting any longer. He couldn't think of a single reason for another test or another dry run or another anything. He had brought this expedition down to the wire and now he had to make his move.

"Okay," he said. "We go!"

29 The prisoner named Raul Maldonada Ramirez was another long-termer who was not enamored of prison life. While he had never been an intimate of Joel Kaplan, his cell was close by and his interest was enormous. Like the others, Ramirez had heard of the rich American's numerous escape attempts. Not without envy, to be sure, for he had nursed a few of his own. Lacking comparable resources, however, he never got very far with his schemes and was forced to content himself with keeping a quiet eye on Kaplan in hopes of finding out his plans, nursing some vague belief that if he did, Kaplan would accept him as a partner.

Ramirez made a habit of observing Kaplan's daily routines as furtively as possible, sometimes lingering unseen by his cell at late hours to hear what might be said between the conspiring roommates. And though he overheard but little, this did not discourage him from his pursuit. Ramirez was not a man to give up easily.

There were even times when he followed Kaplan's third roommate, José Olvera Rico—a fat little man known as "Bad Pedro"—when he went to dispose of their garbage; Ramirez would bring his own garbage along so that his presence might appear innocent. He would then ferret through the Kaplan cell's waste, hoping to find scraps of paper that might give him a clue. A few times, he picked up typewritten letters in English, which had been torn into many shreds; Ramirez would diligently piece these together and, with the aid of a Spanish-English dictionary, manage an adequate translation. Though they related primarily to business matters, the huge sums of money mentioned made his skin flush with excitement. The way he saw it, if he could learn this much by his ingenuity, no doubt he could learn even more by his perseverance. He intensified his spying—though not with such abandon that he risked discovery—concentrating on the garbage whenever possible. This went on for weeks without any success. Then he found a letter that Kaplan had not only torn up but burned as well, and though he could make out little more than the signature "Judy" his mouth went dry with excitement. He began to feel terribly close to Kaplan.

Whenever he saw Kaplan—and he seldom missed a day—his senses became tuned to such a degree that he was afraid to talk to him lest his eagerness give him away. Once he sat across from Joel during a meal, watched the style in which he ate, the way he held his spoon, which foods he ate first, the way he used his bread to push vegetables onto the fork, how much salt and pepper he used. Ramirez began to copy this, having brought himself to that aberrant point of transference wherein he fancied himself to be a man of equal capacities. He began to think in terms of a developing intimacy. At a subsequent meal a few days later, he followed Kaplan into the mess and sat down next to him, this time mustering the courage to speak to him, hoping to begin a dialogue that would lead to a friendship. But Kaplan was neither communicative nor friendly. In fact, he appeared to resent any intrusion on his privacy and acted as though Ramirez did not even exist—or so the man interpreted it.

His frustrations were enormous, so much so that

his admiration and envy quickly turned to scorn. He began to think less of sharing in Kaplan's next escape plan than in its discovery and betrayal. That would be the perfect solution: from *amigo* to *chivato*. Ramirez would expose Kaplan to the Chief of Vigilance and thereby win himself some special favors, perhaps even the shortening of his sentence.

He realized at once that this was a far more reasonable posture for him to take, that it had a much greater likelihood of success. He saw how he'd been a fool to think Kaplan would allow his participation no matter how clever his discovery. In fact, were he to unearth Kaplan's plans and inform him of his discovery, Kaplan no doubt would arrange to have him killed. Had there not been rumors that this was exactly what he had tried to do with the American who worked in the trailer shop?

Reassured now, Ramirez was doubly inspired. He began to keep a written record of what he observed. Exactly how often Kaplan went to dinner, for example. Exactly how often his wife came to visit, at what hours, according to what pattern. What was Kaplan reading, what books, what newspapers? All this was done in consummate detail so that he could immediately note any changes.

That was the key, he knew: the change of routine. When his man was about to do something unique, he would tip it by changing his routine. And that was the time to take special notice.

30 This was the way Vic always wanted it to be: an absolute minimum of waiting. He was going to send that chopper into the courtyard at 6:35, exactly five minutes after Joel and Castro were to begin their walk on the first night scheduled. He was not going to give anyone much of a chance to leak it or anyone else a chance to start guessing about what those two cats were doing out there in the yard walking around with newspapers in their hands.

"You got any questions, Roger?"

"Yeah. How do you fly one of these things?"

"Get in," said Vic, indicating the Cadillac. "I'll teach you on the way back to Pachuca."

"Teach him?" Cotton scowled, extending the gag. "You don't know up from down."

"Cotton, I'll be damned if I didn't hear a woman say that about you."

Vic drove off, listening to Roger's nervous laughter in the seat beside him. The kid was scared, Vic knew. Well, that didn't bother him. A little fear was a good thing, a normal thing. "Show me a man who doesn't get scared and I don't want to have anything to do with him. He ain't real and I wouldn't trust him."

Vic made the twenty-minute run to Pachuca at normal speed, but his mouth was moving at ninety, drawing from his repertoire of experiences a yarn that would lighten Roger's anxiety. Besides, he loved a captive audience. He told the one about the time when he and Pussy were smuggling monkeys and one of the crates broke open and there were four of the things leaping all over the damn airplane. . . .

At Pachuca, there was another fifteen minutes before takeoff, and they sat in the car going over the drill as meticulously as any military operation.

"As soon as you touch down, kick the sandbags out," Vic instructed. The sandbags had been positioned on the rear deck of the chopper to compensate for the ripped-out seats and provide balance; Joel and Castro would hopefully be taking their place. "Then you count to ten seconds. If they aren't aboard, get the hell out of there."

Roger began to practice a ten-second count. "One. Two. Three. Four . . . ." he recited.

"Not that way, that's too fast," interrupted Vic. "Count like this: thousand-and-one, thousand-and-two, thousand-and-three," Roger nodded, understanding. That count was critical.

Vic had clocked it as a forty-two-minute run for the chopper trip from Pachuca to the prison, then fifty-six minutes back to Actopan. Since he wanted the pickup to be made at 6:35, that meant that Roger was to take off at 5:53.

"Ready?" Vic asked.

In all his twenty-nine years, Hershner had never been so keyed up, not even in Vietnam. He was behind the stick in a machine he loved. The cool, damp twilight air was gushing through the open cabin and he was on his way to what had to be the most fantastic thing he had ever done, would probably ever be asked to do. He could see himself back in Glendora having a field day with his buddies as he recounted the entire saga. It was miraculous, all right, the way this caper had come about. It seemed only yesterday that he had begun flying. His big regret was all the years he'd wasted, not even opting for flying when he went into the service. Another two years wasted. But it all ended up roses and maybe it was better this way. He could enjoy it all the more for having waited so long: "Like the way you really appreciate a girl when you're a long time getting to bed with her."

He was over Lake Texcoco now, leading directly to Santa Marta Acatitla. As Cotton had spelled it out, there was no way he could get lost from here. Inside of twelve minutes, he would be at the prison. He checked his watch to verify it: 6:24. He was on schedule, all right. He felt a guarded tightening in his throat as he tried to swallow, reminding him of the urgency of his mission. Needlessly but cautiously, he reviewed his assignment. He would approach the prison from the corner furthest from the guard tower above the main gate, then cross to the first courtyard of the four dormitories. He couldn't miss it. Then he would drop right into its center, being careful to stay clear of the basketball court on the far end. Once he touched down, he would begin counting, thousand-and-one, thousand-and-two, and if by some chance two men carrying newspapers did not appear, he'd take off at the count of ten without them.

And one of the men, he reminded himself, was a murderer.

Joel awoke from his nap slightly later than usual, at about five. "I washed up some, and changed my clothes as I generally do before dinner. Castro had already cleaned up, having spent a few hours with Maribel, and was putting on his money belt. He told me he had sent his new girl to her other man, none other than the Chief of Vigilance himself, thinking that maybe it

216

would be a good idea to keep him occupied for the evening. I had to agree. Good old Maribel, I thought. A regular Mata Hari.

"It was quiet along the cell block. No radio or TV was going. For a moment that bothered me, then I remembered they were showing a movie in the prison theater across the quadrangle. I hadn't thought about that before, but suddenly it seemed like a big plus for us. Everyone was in there watching it, and that would surely make our departure that much simpler, assuming the odd chance that the helicopter would come tonight.

"I boiled some water for tea and, while it was brewing, glanced at the newspapers Irma had brought. In prison I used to get both *El Dià* and *Excelsior*. *El Dià* was the left-wing paper and had the best foreign news. Since it was beginning to rain, I decided to take *Excelsior* with me on the walk. I did not want to soak *El Dià*, I wanted to have it to read that evening if the helicopter didn't show.

"We sipped the tea slowly though it wasn't very hot. We didn't talk. Even Castro was quiet this time. Around 6:20, we picked up our papers and strolled out to the courtyard. Castro took a big stick with him, pretending it was a walking cane. He said he wanted to have some sort of weapon in case anyone else tried to get into the helicopter with us, something to beat them off with.

"For a while I was glad he had it. Even though it was raining, we were suddenly joined by two other prisoners, and I thought, well, maybe the movie had finished. One of them was saying we all ought to go in to eat together, but I said no, not tonight, I had no desire to eat. But he kept insisting. It was 6:30 by then and things were getting sticky, for he had begun to make a dangerous scene, grabbing us as though to tug us in. I didn't understand it. I began to think he knew something was up. I felt that sickening sense that something had gone wrong again, that someone had found out just like before. I saw Castro getting red in the face the way he does when gets angry and I started to worry that he would use that stick, because if he did, there'd be a dozen spectators in a minute, and a half-dozen guards to back them up.

"In the end, it was the rain that saved us. They left, finally, turning up their collars as they walked back inside, muttering something about us that I couldn't quite make out.

"Hoping to stay clear of any others, we walked from the courtyard door toward the basketball court. We stood there in the rain under the backboard, two of the worst athletes who ever made it to Santa Marta, and pretended to discuss shooting baskets. Then Castro said, 'I hear something.' I snapped, 'Nonsense,' though I have rather poor hearing. 'Yes,' he said, 'I hear it coming. Listen!'

"I listened hard, but still heard nothing. Then he saw it, pointing with his stick, and then I saw it, too. It was coming in lower than I would have thought, directly over the dormitory. The rotary was flapping loudly now.

"Within ten or twelve seconds, that's all it took, it was on the ground, and we ran at it, waving the newspapers. We jumped aboard barely a second or two after it touched ground.

"The pilot looked at us and smiled through his beard, his lips moving like a man who was talking to himself, but he stopped as he extended his hand in greeting. 'Hi,' he said. 'My name is Roger Hershner.'

"Hershner turned back to the controls and went on moving his lips. I didn't know what he was saying, but I knew I wanted him to get off the ground fast. I yelled over the noise of the chopper, 'What are we waiting for?' He yelled back, 'Vic told me to count to ten.' Then Hershner nodded as if satisfied and fiddled with the controls. The engine was roaring. You could feel the pent-up power of the ship, just waiting to be unleashed.

218

Then suddenly, there was a tremendous shudder and upward thrust, and we were off the ground.

"I could see the courtyard as we began to climb. A few prisoners had come to the doorway and were staring out at us, their mouths wide open in amazement. Then I saw the one who had followed us out. He was directly below and looking very grim—like a man who has just missed his bus. I waved, just a little flapping of my hand, but he only glared at me. Castro was laughing out loud. I had no trouble hearing that despite all the racket of the rotary. We soared over the tower wall where two guards were standing, watching us go without making a move. I suppose it was because of the official blue coloring. They appeared to be terribly confused. They probably didn't know whether to shoot us or salute.

"The guards had rifles in a rack somewhere nearby, but they never made a move to get them, and even if they had, they wouldn't have had the time to load and shoot. They were supposed to keep a shell or two in their pockets, but, from what I'd heard, such bullets would have been worn so thin over the years just being moved from pocket to pocket that they probably would not have fired anyway.

"I was tempted to wave at them, too, but I didn't. I just sat there and watched the prison wall slip farther and farther away until I could no longer see it.

"The only really frightening moment came when we cleared the wall and the pilot dipped the nose downward to gain speed—for a second I thought we were crashing. For a while we were flying lower than some of the buildings. I could almost reach out and pick leaves off the trees—except that I was afraid to because there were no doors and I figured I might fall out.

"I can remember thinking only one thing: this was my first helicopter ride."

31

The prisoner closest to the escaping helicopter was none other than Raul
Maldonada Ramirez, the unfortunate
neighbor of Kaplan and Castro who had so diligently
sought to betray them. On that final evening of
Wednesday, August 18, Ramirez had waited for Kaplan
as he usually did to see if he were going in for dinner.
On this evening, he suspected that Kaplan would, for
neither he nor Castro had eaten since noon, sharing
merely a pot of tea. Ramirez wasn't sure why, but he had
a feeling that something was up. He had even chosen to
skip the afternoon movie—*Altar of Blood*—in order to
stay close at hand.

At 6:25, he was still dallying in his cell, stalling his
own cellmate as he kept an eye on the neighboring cell
across the hallway; then seeng the two come out, he
followed them, thinking they were going to the mess
hall. After all, Kaplan had his jacket on, the one he
generally wore when he ate in the mess.

Instead, they turned the other way, out to the courtyard.

Ramirez did not know what to make of it and, as
though magnetized, proceeded to follow them out, his
own cellmate alongside. A curious scene, Ramirez
thought. What were they doing in the yard, both with

220

their rolled up newspapers? It had even begun to rain. Kaplan was certainly not one to walk in the rain, certainly not so soon after his operation. For a moment, Ramirez stood in the doorway watching, irritated now by his cellmate who was trying to draw him away. Forced to make a move of some sort, Ramirez walked out into the yard directly in front of Kaplan. And when Kaplan and Castro started to move away, he followed them, attempting to force a conversation.

"Say, aren't you two coming in to dinner?"

"No." It was Castro who replied.

"Come on, we're inviting you for a free meal."

"Not tonight, thank you."

They were walking away from the dormitory toward the basketball court, and Ramirez's cellmate began to pull his arm, advising him that they didn't have that much time for dinner, obviously unaware of what was happening here, all the more preposterous to him because of the rain. Ramirez, facing the oddity of Kaplan's conduct, recognized the oddity of his own, and not wishing to create undue suspicion by his own actions, decided to oblige his cellmate. He moved away, but not without noticing that Kaplan had turned up his collar against the inclement weather. As he hurried across the yard to the door, he wondered what meaning that had.

Inside now, he stalled again, this time on the pretext that he had to return to his cell to put on a dry jacket. He would later estimate that not more than a minute had passed when he heard vaguely familiar sounds from outside, but since there were no windows in his cell, it reached his ears muffled by brick walls and closed doors. Nonetheless, he reacted quickly, hurrying out of his cell, down the corridor, and out to the courtyard.

Then he saw it, a huge blue helicopter sitting on the stone pavement, its rotary spinning above like a giant fan. And there was Kaplan climbing aboard, Castro already inside. Ramirez raced toward them with no other thought than to be with them, somehow believing he had earned that right. Indeed, the helicopter appeared to remain there for an added second or two as though it were actually waiting for him.

When he got there, it was still on the ground, and he lunged for the opening, only to have a large stick thrust at him; before he could grab hold of the doorway, the machine suddenly leaped into the air like a frightened horse, literally throwing him to the ground.

When he looked up, he saw Kaplan waving, but he was too stunned to react.

Martin Salinas Rodriguez was one of the more than a hundred guards at Santa Marta Acatitla Prison, and according to all reports and investigations that would begin on the following day, he was the only one who saw it happen.

"I looked through the window of the dormitory corridor when I heard this strange noise of the machine. I thought, what is happening, what is going on here? Then I saw a little gray [sic] helicopter sitting in the middle of the yard. Then I saw Contreras Castro and behind him Kaplan running toward it. I realized then that this was to be an escape, so I ran down the hall screaming, 'Shoot! Shoot!' "

Rodriguez was a hefty man, somewhat overweight at forty-one, slow of mind as well as body. Had he been as resourceful as he was loud, he might have circled Dormitory Number One and reached the yard of Dormitory Number Two, where the nearest guard tower, without a view into the yard of Number One, could have been warned—perhaps in time to fire on the departing chopper. Instead, he ran out to the yard of Number One.

"When I got to the yard, I was able to see Kaplan take off. I shouted with all my strength: 'They're running away, they're running away, somebody shoot them!' but nobody did. I kept pulling my hair because I was not armed. I'm not a bad shot. I ran back to the guard room hollering at the Guard Alvaro, 'Alvaro, they're escaping!' He picked up the telephone to report what was happening to the Chief of Vigilance, but the line was busy. I ran to the main office to sound the alarm. Why wasn't I armed! Inside the prison, no guard is armed. Only on the walls, in the towers, and nobody was doing a thing, nobody."

Roger Hershner was proud of the chopper. It had handled the drop and the climb perfectly, its engine taking the extraordinary stress of the 200 rpm over Red Line as it sat there waiting, then driving into the thin air without a trace of stuttering. Following Vic's instructions, he moved away from the prison keeping as low as he could, once too close, as he felt the landing gear brush against the upper limbs of some trees. The plan was to keep low, out of range of radar and remain out of sight for as long as possible. It was getting dark, which would help. It would also make the route back to Actopan a lot harder to follow.

32

There was a gate at the landing field at Actopan, the only entrance to the huge area that, because it also served duty as a cow pasture, was surrounded by a rickety fence. Vic had backed the Cadillac into that gate to block any intruders. The Cessna 210, once again with its original registration number showing, waited a few yards away at the beginning of what might laughingly be called a runway. But then, both Vic and Cotton had landed and taken off on a lot worse.

The three, Vic, Cotton, and the blonde, sat in the Caddy and waited, trapped by the drizzle that had begun to fall, an hour of interminable minutes during which they had absolutely nothing to do but sweat.

Suddenly—the honk of an automobile horn. Vic wheeled in his seat as a pickup truck flashed its headlights outside the gate, obviously wanting to get by the Cadillac and enter the field. Vic got out of the Caddie to see what to make of it, but not before checking his watch again. It was 7:16. The chopper was due in sixteen minutes.

The pickup had two men in it, and on its door was a federal seal having something to do with aeronautics. Vic had never seen that seal before, but Mexico was loaded with all kinds of officials—they came in all colors, he liked to say. The question was, what were this man's real colors at the moment? What did he want here? Vic had used the field a dozen times and had never seen an official car there before.

The Commandante, as he called himself, indicated that he wanted to come in, then explained that he was checking to see that there were no cows on the runway. Vic smiled casually, moving the Caddie from the entrance. The pickup drove slowly by, the men inside taking a long look at the Caddie, the blonde, and then the 210. Vic watched them drive down the fence line, still moving very slowly, no more than 5 mph. The truck turned around at the far end of the runway and parked facing them with its headlights on.

It was clear that they weren't looking for any cows.

"I don't like it," said Vic.

"As long as they stay where they are," said Cotton.

"They didn't like the Caddie and the 210 too much. But wait till they see the chopper," Vic said. Then he added his own little fear: "I'd like to see it myself."

It was not yet 7:30, still a few minutes to go, but there was something brutally ominous stirring and Vic was beginning to have a bad time of it. He couldn't get back in the Caddie now, not with his mind conjuring up images of a dozen cars moving onto the field, all of them sporting damn Mexican insignia on the door; and, when the chopper landed, all those doors would open and a hundred men with carbines would surround them. He'd had that nightmare more than a few times. The fact he'd lived through it seemed irrelevant now. He moved to the Caddie shakier than he'd felt in years.

Vic began staring up at the sky, peering through the night mist for a light, straining his ears for that special sound. It was 7:35 and there was still nothing.

"They're late," he said.

He turned toward the headlights across the field. Every minute that went by made that pickup truck more threatening, and Vic began to consider going over there and talking to the two men in it; perhaps he could find out if they knew something—maybe there'd been a police report from Santa Marta about the escape in a chopper; maybe all airfields were alerted.

"Then I thought, no, that wasn't possible. Not a chance, not yet, at any rate. He was just a Mexican official who'd stumbled into a situation here. He would sit there and wait the way Mexican cops always do. Like a bull. He'd watch and wait like a bull, trying to decide whether to attack or retreat, it would all depend on how he sized up the situation. The thing to do was wait him out."

If the bull decided to charge, however, well, that was something else. Vic would have to take action, one way or another. A bribe, perhaps. He could slip him $10. . . . Give him $20 and he'd climb a tree for you. But if he didn't—if the bribe looked like it would backfire, as they sometimes do—he'd have to use stronger means. And this, too, was not an unfamiliar procedure for him. He and Cotton "had been through enough scrapes to write a damned good TV series." They tried to avoid violence wherever possible, "but we'd handcuffed more than a few commandantes to a fencepost or a tree. I never once hurt one, though there were a few times I wouldn't have minded breaking an arm."

The seconds ran like hours now.

"It was terrible. I was ready to believe anything, like the chopper had blown up trying to get off the ground . . . or that Castro did something to louse it up. Jesus, at that moment I hated him as much as I hated choppers. It was the waiting that did it. Hell, if I'd actually been doing something, I'd never have gotten so jittery.

"Then I heard it. Flop-flop-flop. He was coming, all right, about three minutes late.

"But he was heading for the wrong end of the field, flying straight toward the Commandante's headlights!

If he landed there, he'd be handing Joel over to the goddamn officials!

"I raced to the Cessna and flashed on its landing lights, on and off, on and off, and then the rotating blinker on top. Roger spotted them and reversed his direction, and all of a sudden I had another crazy fear that he was coming back alone. I stared hard, trying to see inside the cabin but it was too damned dark. But then, like an answer to a prayer, there was a brilliant streak of lightning and the chopper lit up as if a spotlight had hit it—and there they were, the two passengers, sitting behind Roger like a couple of jerks on a joy ride. I jumped for the Cessna.

"He dropped the chopper a few yards away from me. Joel came running out and climbed straight into the Cessna, just as he'd been told to do, and then Castro tried to do the same, just as he'd been told not to. I shouted at him, 'No, no, goddamnit, go to the Caddie,' but he wouldn't listen. I pushed him out and he climbed back in, so I pushed him out again. Old Cotton finally had to grab him and stuff him into the car.

"I finally got the door of the Cessna locked, waved at Roger, and gunned the engine, moving straight at the Commandante's headlights to line up the takeoff, and suddenly I had one of those godawful flashes that the sonovabitch was going to put that pickup in gear and come charging at me like a goddamn bull. I'd had that happen enough times, a crazy kind of chicken run when you dare each other to keep coming, car against plane. I remembered once on a level mountain top. It was another truck, not a car—they never come in cars the way cops are supposed to, that would be too suspicious looking; they cruise around in trucks like a bunch of hard-working farmers or something. But I had my contraband loaded and began my takeoff and they drove the damn pickup right at me. Jesus, they kept coming and I kept coming, it was a suicide deal. They usually turn off because a plane can hardly do the same, but this one didn't, and I just barely climbed over it as they jumped out of the truck as it was about to hit.

"But this time, the Commandante just sat there. So we took off bumping along at 60 mph, I was afraid of blowing a tire on that rough terrain—that's all we need now, I thought. But up we went, right over the Commandante, and we hadn't gone 200 feet when we hit a goddamn storm that rocked us halfway back to Mother Earth. Lightning to the right, lightning to the left. But we were heading north, by God.

"I handed Joel the bottle of Scotch, and he took a good swig of it.

"Then he turned to me and said it all in five little words: 'Excellent. The timing was excellent!'"

33 The storm continued to rage around them. Vic took the plane up to 14,000 feet on the assumption that they'd be safe at that altitude, but suddenly there were towering mountains directly to the west. "Joel had been working on that Scotch, but when I saw those hills—by God, they weren't supposed to be there!—I almost demanded a slug of that juice myself." He was having difficulty keeping a radio contact with the Pachuca airport, another unnerving problem, but finally managed to find the Tampico beam, guiding himself north accordingly. They were about thirty miles west of Tampico when they broke out of the storm and saw the city twinkling below.

From there it was a simple matter to head toward Brownsville. Vic immediately established radio contact to let them know he was coming, wanting to secure the legality of their entrance by having it recorded from miles away. Not trusting any official anywhere, he did not want to give them a chance to say later that he had sneaked across the border or made an illegal landing in some hidden Texas field. He kept talking back and forth to them, forcing a stupid conversation at the risk of irritating them.

A legal arrival for Vic Stadter. But how legal was his passenger?

The ninth inning was coming up. What was about to happen was everything. Nothing that had preceded his arrival at Brownsville mattered now. If he had won all the little battles of his escape, they would come to nothing at this final confrontation because of a single "if":

If the Immigration Officer decided to send Joel back across the border.

It could happen. Vic knew it to the very guts of him. It was almost 9 o'clock in the evening, barely two-and-a-half hours since they'd plucked the prisoner from the Santa Marta courtyard. Had the prison officials announced the escape? Had the Mexican Government contacted all border Immigration offices?

Vic led Joel into the Brownsville Customs and Immigration Office and stared into the face of the last enemy, a wormy little man in his late fifties, tired and bored and harrassed after twenty-five years pushing troubled people around. "He looked like he hadn't been laid in the last ten," Vic remembers thinking, picturing the joy on the man's face if he took Joel into custody, then shoved him back across the border to his soul brother, the Mexican Customs and Immigration official.

What Vic hated most was that this was America, and the man was an American official supposedly there to represent Americans, but you couldn't trust him for any of that.

This was the confrontation most vital to the entire scheme of Joel's escape. The multimillion dollar estate had dictated the terms: Joel had to be legally admitted to the United States. This precluded another sort of re-entrance, one that Vic could have arranged more safely, for the Mexican-American border is a vast one, easily penetrated, especially by air, and doubly easy at night.

This was, then, the million-dollar gamble. All or nothing, as it were. And now, right now, they were going to take one big juicy roll of the dice.

"Well, well, if it isn't the great Mr. Stadter."

Sure, there it was, the snide challenge for openers. It's Vic Stadter coming in from Mexico, boys, at night, no less, and one look at that plane of his showed how hard he'd been pushing it. One thing was certain, there had to be some contraband around.

"And to what do we owe the pleasure of your company?" the man asked, just like a sleazy TV movie when the bad guy has the good guy cornered and wants to have a little fun with him before he cuts him up.

"We're a couple of tired fellas, Mister," Vic offered. "We'd like to get cleared so we can get on our way."

"Who's he?" the official said, barely looking at Joel.

Well, here we go, Vic thought. Now we're going to play the big scene. One look at that name on the birth certificate and the jackal was going to jump sky high. Vic could picture that sneering triumphant face, like a guy who just found buried treasure. Well, well, the man would say, look who's here, damned if I didn't get a little old call about you, not fifteen minutes ago.

Joel reached into his pocket and instead of the fresh identification Vic had so carefully prepared for him, he held out his frayed and crumpled naval discharge from 1946. The man glanced at the paper, then handed it back. When he looked up, it was the same old angry face, totally without joy. Vic couldn't have loved him more.

"What's he doing with you, Stadter?" he asked.

Vic let out air, unable to contain his relief. "He's a cotton grower. We met in Mexico City—"

"Suppose we take a look at your plane," the man broke in, completely indifferent to Joel's presence.

"Be my guest," said Vic.

They looked. They stripped it down, then finding

nothing, they went back and stripped it down again. In typically expert fashion, they looked through every conceivable hiding place, feeding their frustration as they did. And when they returned to the office, Vic would see the official's rage. Somehow, he had been foiled and there wasn't a damn thing he could do about it.

Except to keep them there for a while longer.

This was what frightened Vic. Again, time was the enemy. If they stalled him long enough, the news of the escape was likely to come through. He figured that they had a certain amount of leeway, but he didn't know how much. His guess was that the guards would immediately report Joel's escape to the warden, but the warden would be slow to report it to higher authorities. It would be too humiliating for him, knowing that the consequences were certain to be disastrous. His reactions, then, were apt to be extremely cautious and calculating, half working out a course of action to create a fall guy, and half hoping that somehow Joel Kaplan would turn up for roll call in the morning.

"It was a very squirrelly time," said Vic. Every time the phone rang—which it did, repeatedly—he could feel the sweat form on his neck. And each time it rang again, he actually had that gut-wrenching sense of doom; this time it would be some big official calling to advise that an escaped prisoner named Joel David Kaplan was wanted by the Mexican Government and was probably heading toward the border.

Joel, meanwhile, had returned to the bench in a distant corner, pale, unkempt, dirty-bearded, pathetic. He sat with his right leg draped over his left, hands folded in front of him, looking like an unemployed schoolteacher whose wife had just left him.

Vic began to wonder what he would do if the news came through while he and Joel waited. He really didn't know. Though he had a horrible sense that it was going to happen, he had no idea what he would do. The options were all inadequate—like threatening the official with exposure to the Brownsville newspapers: the American Immigration Official who had handed a fellow citizen back to the Mexicans after he had pulled off a fantastic escape. He would name the man, by God, so that everyone would know what an un-American bastard he was, blackening his name so his own kids wouldn't talk to him. Of course, it wouldn't work, and Vic knew it: this was a man who enjoyed doing things like that; a man who loved his work, he'd have it all figured out how he was obeying orders, that's all. Oh, Vic would ride on him for that, too, reminding him how every goddamn big shot official who ordered him to do it would deny he even knew about it the next day, it would all be dumped on him, he'd be left holding the bag for it. But Vic knew that the bastard would just laugh at him. "Hell, the way they'd set it up, you'd never be able to prove we had him across the border in the first place!"

There was also the bribe. He could go to him and convince him that the game could be played the other way too. Since no one would admit that Joel had made it into the United States, here's a thousand bucks to forget about the whole thing.

But that, too, would never work, not with this jackal, not because he was honest but because he was afraid someone would rat on him.

So Vic stood there sweating, listening to half a phone conversation, as meek as a mouse, by God, and that pasty-faced old sonovabitch was spinning his wheels looking for some traction.

"All right, you two, take off your clothes," he barked.

Another stall, Vic thought, considerably relieved. Examine the clothes, then examine the body. See if anything was hidden that might be contraband.

It wasn't until they'd come to the frustrating end of this round that the mouse named Stadter squeaked back at the jackal.

"That's some great job you got, Mister, trying to find your answers up another man's asshole."

It was the greatest insult that he could have made, but the official was not about to break his stride. He looked daggers at Vic and began muttering profanities of his own. One thing was clear: he wasn't a quitter.

Joel sat wearily back in his corner. It had been a long day. It promised to be longer.

"You okay, Dan?" Vic asked him.

Joel nodded.

"Dan? It says here his name is Joel," the official snapped. Neither Vic nor Joel said a word, and the man pursued it like a sleuth on the verge of some earth-shaking discovery. "Okay, Stadter, what's this 'Dan' business?"

Vic scowled at his own blunder, warned himself not to get careless now and compound it. Like a seasoned in-fighter, he sensed it was a moment to defy, not back away.

"'Dan.' I call him 'Dan.' What's the big deal?"

"It ain't his name, that's what."

"So it's a nickname."

"I thought you said you just met him in Mexico City."

"I called you 'Judas' the day I met you."

"Goddammit, Stadter, just what are you up to?"

Vic began to laugh, suddenly remembering the old smugglers' joke about the guy who kept hauling a wheelbarrow full of manure across the border, and the Customs official kept probing through it looking for contraband until this daily routine drove him up a tree. Finally, he said to the smuggler: "Look, I'll make a deal with you; just tell me what you're smuggling and I won't stop you again." "Sure," said the smuggler; "it's wheelbarrows!"

The official went back to his desk and went fumbling for a large pad to join his ballpoint pen. He was ready to quit the body and shift to the mouth—ques-

234

tions, this time, another ruse to mark time. Name . . .
date of birth . . . place of birth . . . schooling . . . marital
status . . . children . . . occupation . . . organization
. . . previous arrests and convictions.

"You can't ask that!" snapped the little man sitting
on the bench.

"What do you mean, why not?" the official was
stunned at Joel's challenge.

"The law does not permit that question. If a man
has served time for a crime, he has paid for it. He is not
required to put it on your record."

The jackal was intimidated, whatever the validity
of Joel's claim. At the moment, it was all Vic needed.
He had served enough time himself on that other "goddamn government frame-up" and he was not going to
suffer this bastard to push him around any more.

"All right, dammit," Vic snapped, "you've had your
little fun. We've been here an hour and a half. You've
found nothing inside or outside my asshole so you got
no reason to hold us. Now clear these papers and let
us get out of here!"

There was nothing the official could come up with
that would justify holding onto the two any longer. He
looked at Stadter and had to concede defeat, a look
that Vic knew all too well. So Vic took his "wheelbarrow" back into the Cessna with him, not saying another
word. He needed gas, but he didn't want to hang around
Brownsville for another minute.

No sooner did he become airborne, turning the
plane west across Texas, when he let out a cry that
appeared to shake the plane in its flight. It was a cry of
relief and joy and triumph. It sent shivers down his
own spine, his emotion was so great.

They had done it, by Christ! They had done it all!

"You're free, you crazy bastard, you're FREE!"

And he began to laugh, tremendous laughter, laughter that made his eyes tear and his chest heave,
laughter that left him spluttering like the village idiot,

235

on and on he laughed, the ludicrousness of it feeding Joel's own laughter, a laughter suddenly so meaningful that he was crying with it, genuine tears as uncontrollable as the joy that had brought them on.

Joel reached down for the bottle of Old Smuggler and unscrewed the cap.

"Here," he said, "I think you need a drink."

Part Five

HELIFUGITIVES

34

The landing field at Actopan, from the vantage point of the Commandante in the pickup truck, was a mad skirmish of landing and takeoff, of passengers racing from one machine to another in three different carriers moving out in three different directions. Even before Vic had gone barreling down that bumpy runway in the 210, Cotton, the blonde, and Roger Hershner had the chopper loaded with fuel cans, blankets, food. And even before Roger had the chopper off the ground again, Cotton, with Vic's blonde in the front seat and Contreras Castro in the back, was swinging his Baroque Bronze Cadillac through the gate.

The entire operation, from Hershner's dramatic return to their complete departure, could not have taken more than two minutes.

Vic said later: "Hell, we'd been there long enough."

Cotton had been instructed to take Castro to the nearest "decent" town and deposit him at a hotel with orders to remain under cover until contacted. They ended up around midnight, 200 miles away in San Luis Potosi. It had not been a dull ride for Cotton. He'd had the radio going, worrying over the news reports. Not a word was mentioned. Castro propped his arms across the rear of the front seat and kept jabbering away, a nonstop run that was only occasionally interrupted by a bit of nuzzling into the back of the blonde's neck. She didn't seem to mind.

San Luis Potosi was a good-sized town of 275,000 population, not a bad town to get lost in. Cotton pulled up at the Hotel Panorama, gave Castro $500, an empty suitcase, and a name (José Gonzales). Then he added some advice: button up your big fat mouth. But he knew there was no way the garrulous Venezuelan could possibly do that. Castro had that maddening what-the-hell quality to him, a seeming indifference to his fate. It was as if the only thing that mattered was how he could use his mouth, more for what came out of it than what he could put in.

"La Boca Grande," Vic had labeled him.

As he pulled out of town en route north, Cotton could taste his relief at being left with the blonde and the radio. He drove all night, stopping only for gas and coffee. When he crossed the Rio Grande into Laredo, it was already daylight. There was still no radio news, and as a result, there was no hassling with Customs and Immigration.

Two of the three machines were safely back.

The third was the $65,000 helicopter.

Immediately after he had brought Joel and Castro into Actopan, Roger had scrambled out, his rotary twirling, grabbed the maps, papers, blanket, and food that Vic had prepared for him. He saw Vic barely long enough to note his gesture to get out of there immediately, one of those changes in plan Vic was always quick to improvise. Roger knew it had something to do with that eerie pair of headlights at the far end of the field, and almost as quickly as Vic began his takeoff

240

and Cotton hauled away in the Caddie, Roger took the chopper up and away.

Roger had planned to stay overnight at Actopan, not wanting to fly in the dark in unfamiliar territory. The exultation of his successful rescue was quickly replaced by the feeling that he was in far more trouble than he deserved. The weather was socking him in, winds, rain, heavy clouds, lightning—everything he hated. He had a vague idea he was flying up a ravine as he felt his way around the area. It was the lightning that eventually saved him: he saw what looked like a landing spot in that quick flash of light and turned toward it, carefully lowering his craft between a grouping of large trees and some uneven ground. He was proud of his landing and not just a little sorry that there was no one with him to impress.

He was tired but too exhilarated to sleep, nor did the open cabin of the chopper afford a warm and comfortable spot. He awoke from an intermittent sleep long before dawn, drank his fruit juice, and impatiently waited for the first trace of daylight. He was up and heading north considerably before sunrise.

He located his first homemade refuelling depot hidden by a small lake, carefully situated away from all roads, high in the hills. Roger began to feel better about his prospects, having executed this leg of his trek to the border despite the difficult weather. Again, he was proud of his navigation as well as his skill as a pilot. As he poured the gas into the tank, he told himself he would celebrate with a bottle of champagne when he got to Brownsville, even if he had only himself to celebrate with. Then he heard a sound behind him and he turned his head. What he saw was so startling "I didn't know whether to piss or go blind."

A band of Indians on horseback, perhaps a dozen men, were standing in a semicircle around him. They said nothing, barely moved, in fact, just watched with that menacing inscrutableness that would frighten any

American who had ever seen a Hollywood movie. Roger was not impressed by their reluctance to attack, especially since their leaders were sporting shotguns. He felt that chilling onset of panic, remembering vague words of warning from Vic about how Indians might shoot at him on this adventure but not to worry because they were such lousy shots. A joke, he had thought, one of those ribbings that old hands like to dish out to neophytes. But now it was real, and there was no way they could possibly miss him from this distance, no way at all. He shuddered and stopped thinking, and his body did the work for him. He dropped the can of gas and leaped into the chopper, hoping that the roar of the engine would intimidate them, and he lifted the powerful machine in record time—so fast that all his maps, charts, instructions, and identification papers blew helter-skelter out of the open cabin.

He didn't care. He was alive and gone before anyone had time to draw a bead on him. As Vic had told him repeatedly, you had to face each problem as you came to it. He found the second stash of fuel at Ajascador ("that right tight hole in the jungle") without anything to guide him but his instincts. Incredibly, Roger found it on his first approach, remembering the shape of a jagged peak a few hundred yards to the east. He thought then that the smart thing to do was head for the Atlantic coastline and follow it north from La Pesca to Brownsville. It was longer, but more certain of direction. Pleased with this decision, he turned to the northeast, keeping as low as possible to avoid radar detection.

His troubles were only beginning, however, for the engine began to overheat, forcing him to make repeated landings. Then, as he reached the coast just above La Pesca, he noted a plane flying overhead at about 7,000 feet, keeping to the same route as he. The way Roger saw it, the police were assuming that Kaplan was aboard and were keeping tabs on him. He began to picture them pursuing him with military aircraft. To evade them, his helicopter mind went to work for him, and he eventually found a landing spot on the narrow peninsular along the Laguna Madre, so inaccessible that no one could reach him, even with another chopper. As soon as he landed, he worked beaver-like hauling branches and shrubs to camouflage the craft.

That done, he immediately went to work on the engine, knowing that time was beginning to press him, that the longer he remained in Mexico, the more difficult would be his return across the border. Hampered by a total lack of repair equipment, he attacked the engine with the desperation of a surgeon trying to remove a brain tumor with an old penknife. Luck, however, was with him. In time, he saw what had happened: when he had made that hurried getaway from the Indians, one of his windblown charts had flown directly into the cooling fan and jammed it. It was a simple operation after all.

He spent the night there, vaguely hoping all his troubles would disappear by morning. With luck, he could move out at dawn. He figured it as no more than a two-hour run to the border. With a little more luck, he should be able to cross without pursuit.

He was up in the air again at daybreak, but inside of an hour, he saw a plane overhead again, and he knew he was in for it. Troubles compounded by troubles. Vic had instructed him about recrossing the border legally, especially now, after the escape. This meant checking in with the Brownsville Customs office, using the special frequency all aircraft were required to use, having it recorded on official U.S. radio, taped as he spoke, checked in by radar. As Vic had put it: "When push comes to shove in this affair, those government workers are going to find the weakest link in the chain and attack it for all it's worth. You can't give them any chances. See to it that it all gets down in the records and they'll have to rat on each other instead of on you."

Roger suffered through the memory of it for he had

lost all his instructions on how to make such radio contact. The closer he came to the border, the more helpless he felt. He was running scared now and he couldn't think properly. That plane hovering overhead all the way made him think of the police. It had to be police. If he flew into Brownsville, they'd be there waiting for him. Instead of Indians, there'd be a dozen Immigration Officials awaiting his landing.

He decided not to fly into Brownsville but to find another hiding place. He took the chopper up high enough to see the border city of Matamoros, then turned tail toward the city until he picked out a clearing among a large cluster of trees on the outskirts of town.

Vic had told him that, if he had to abandon ship, he was to put a hole in the gas tank, set a light to it, and burn the damn thing up. It was safer not to leave any evidence behind. Roger considered it but took the law of survival into his own hands. A burning helicopter was bound to draw attention to him. Somehow, he hoped he could remain anonymous. Besides, he "loved the damn thing." So he did the next best thing: he tried to camouflage its existence as he had the day before. It was like trying to conceal a dead whale in a trout pond.

It would be difficult to judge how many people had seen the chopper around Matamoros before it had made its descent. Doubtlessly, there were dozens. One, for certain, was a ten-year-old boy who lived not a mile from the landing site, and he immediately ran to tell his parents. They were not surprised, then, when a bearded American appeared at their door seeking advice as to how he might get to Matamoros and from there across the border into the United States.

Roger was well-treated. It was a peasant's home with little more than the barest necessities. They offered him coffee and spoke enough English to tell him that the milk truck would be along shortly, and perhaps he could hitch a ride into town on it. He thanked them all profusely as this was duly arranged, and no one mentioned the helicopter supposedly hidden in the woods. He was, in fact, so exceptionally well-treated that he began to suspect a trap.

Arriving at Matamoros in the milk truck, his suspicions soared. Was he being driven not to the border but to a police station? He did not care to find out. When the driver stopped at a traffic light, Roger indicated that he had to make a phone call, pointing to the sidewalk booth. The driver nodded and pulled his truck to a parking place, which was not at all what Roger had suggested or wished. Nonchalantly, he went to the phone and feigned the dialing as he watched the driver chat with a group of Mexicans not a dozen yards away. One of them nodded and moved quickly into an adjacent building, and that was all Roger needed to see. He immediately left the phone booth and hurried to other streets around other corners, trying to disappear into the local hubbub. He spotted a taxi, got in, and told the driver to take him to the border. The driver, however, was devastatingly inexperienced, constantly stalling in traffic and failing to execute the proper turns. At one point, the taxi created a mammoth traffic jam at a narrow intersection, and Roger himself had to help the unfortunate and intimidated driver out of it.

He caught another taxi and this time managed to get across the Rio Grande, knowing that his troubles were far from over. Indeed, the way he saw it, he had merely traded one set of problems for another.

He presented himself at Customs without any of the proper papers, having lost them all to the Indians. Yet the example of the man named Victor E. Stadter had not been lost on him. Roger played his bearded hippie appearance to the hilt, bluffing, lying, cajoling the already harassed official with talk of transcendental woes that more than explained his lack of an ID, and he moved through the entry line like an old pro.

Two days later, the chopper was loaded on a huge trailer flat bed, then escorted through town by the Mexican Judiciales as though they had captured a trophy of war.

It finally came to rest in a section of the Mexico City Airport where helicopters—including that other blue copter used by the Attorney General—were stored.

35

Vic brought the Cessna down at McAllen Airfield, some fifty miles from Brownsville. The craft needed refueling, and besides, they were exhausted.

They checked into the motel adjacent to the airfield, and Joel had his first chance to call his sister, who was now living in Santa Fe.

"Hi, this is Joel."

"No kidding."

"Can't you recognize my voice?"

"Sure, but where are you?"

"Texas."

"You mean Acatitla."

"Judy, we made it! Vic flew me out. We made it!"

"Sure, but how come I don't believe you?"

It took a few more words from Vic to convince her. There was no way the two of them could be talking on the same phone unless the impossible were true.

"Well, I'll be a sonovabitch!" she said.

Irma Vasquez Calderon Kaplan didn't believe it either. There had been so many false reports, broken promises and betrayals, so many disappointments—she could not be burdened by the emotion of another.

"That's nice," she said when one of Vic's Mexico City contacts called with the news of the escape. "Tell him to bring home some milk for the baby."

Then she went to bed.

An hour later, there was a knock on her door. She opened it to fifteen Mexican policemen. They entered the apartment she shared with her mother and the baby. "They really thought Joel was there. The first thing they did was to look under the bed!"

She found herself laughing at the impact of such a Marx Brothers situation. She stopped laughing when they insisted that she go to the police station for interrogation. Defiantly, she took her dog and cats along with her while her mother stayed with the baby. But she was frightened, not knowing if Joel had made it all the way.

"I think the police were enjoying the escape. Someone else was going to be in hot water for a change. I asked them, 'Why don't you put me in jail too?' and they said 'No, you'd fly out in a helicopter and then we'd be in trouble too.' "

She was put through a long, trying night in front of a battery of police investigators and newspaper reporters, not knowing where one group ended and the other began. Though she became weary and harassed, she remained proud and defiant.

"Put me in jail, but I tell you nothing!" she taunted them. "I don't know anything about it. I don't know who planned the escape and I don't know who carried it off. I know nothing. If I did, do you think I'd be around here to be captured by you people?"

That last was not entirely true. She wouldn't have been sitting there if she'd followed instructions.

"I demand to be released: all this questioning is arbitrary and useless. I've done nothing, and you know it. I want to go home. I insist you let me go home!"

They kept her for hours, reminding her that she had been there at the prison that very morning before her husband had escaped. She didn't need reminding and she told them so. Yes, she had been there, just the way she usually was there. And yes, she had come with a man named Harvey Orville Dail, having picked him up at the Holiday Inn. No, she did not know what business Señor Dail had with her husband. Her husband's business was not her business and she had stayed apart from them as they talked.

"Irma Kaplan is small," the reporters wrote, "but she has a very strong character."

It was not until 6 A.M. on August 19, 1971, almost twelve hours after the escape, that Irma learned Joel was safe. She was in the office of Sam Lopez, the Police Chief of Mexico City. Chief Lopez was a very disgruntled man, and the phone call he received with Irma sitting in front of his desk did little to improve his humor.

"That dirty fucking gringo has crossed the border," the chief shouted to his aide, slamming down the receiver.

36

Santa Marta Acatitla Prison was swarming with important officials, most of whom were law enforcement people representing the brass: Local, Federal, Secret, Highway Patrol, Air Patrol, even the Mexican Mounties. The butt of all their scorn were such leading prison authorities as Acatitla's director, José Luis Campos Burgos, Captain Andres Dueñas Sosa of the Department of Vigilance, and Major Martinez, his Chief of Vigilance at Acatitla. The first response was to seal off the prison to prevent any of its personnel from leaving. All the guards and most other prison employees were detained through the night for investigation, as it was officially stated that this escape could not have taken place without the complicity of the prison guards and, most probably, a number of officials.

What then followed must stand as a case history in the art of the alibi. Fabrications piled upon buck-passing piled upon suspicion—all resulting in a sprawling mass of contradictions:

Tower guard Ramiro Hernandez Medina claimed that, when he saw the helicopter land, he set off the alarm system but it did not work.

(The system was tested by the warden's staff shortly thereafter and was perfectly operative, although

no guard questioned could recall when the alarm system had last been checked or when there had been drills.)

Victoriano Cruz Lopez, a guard in the main watch tower along the helicopter's line of flight, declared that he did not fire his machine gun because it had jammed. He was then put into custody for failure to report an inoperative weapon.

(*Subsequently, the police revealed that the machine gun in question was in perfect order.*)

Other guards stated that they did not shoot since they were told that the helicopter had landed because of mechanical problems.

(*Officials denied saying any such thing.*)

Officials claimed that the helicopter pilot was directed to the correct yard by a guard who had been paid off.

(*No one knew which guard this was.*)

An Inspector from the Secret Service claimed that Kaplan had not escaped by helicopter but in a totally different way.

(*He was taken to the yard and shown two large sandbags [dumped from the chopper] and an oil spot some fifty centimeters in diameter. He then conceded his error.*)

The one claim that makes the most sense is the guards' statements that they did not shoot, believing this was a visit by a high government official.

Newspaper reporters noted this preposterous parade and wrote accordingly: "Santa Marta is supposed to be escape-proof, with the largest equipment in alarm systems and well-armed guards in perfectly placed towers. However, nothing seems to have worked. Not a single shot was fired. Here were two prisoners, both of whom had tried to escape before; one of whom, Joel Kaplan, had made several attempts at bribery; but there was no one around to watch them because they were all at the movies; they didn't even see them leave!"

Wrote another: "The entire staff was detained overnight. Prisoners were not permitted in any yard. The Mounties surrounded the prison walls in a fully armed parade to prevent anyone from getting out—except Kaplan and Castro, who had already left."

Sections XXI and XLVI of Article 18 of the Mexican Penal Code deal with complicity or failure to prevent an escape, failure to communicate with superiors about knowledge of a possible escape. Director of Investigations Luis Porte Petit revealed that the guards were liable to a sentence of five years in prison for their negligence. He made no mention of officials.

Mexican police officials asked the help of the U.S. Federal Bureau of Investigation for the capture and return of the two prisoners. It was believed that both had escaped to the United States.

The Mexican Air Force and border patrols were alerted to a Cessna 210, registration 8482X, which was presumably on its way south to Guatemala, carrying the escaped prisoner Contreras Castro en route to his home in Venezuela.

Reporters were permitted in Cell Number 10 where Kaplan's other cellmate, José Guadalupe Olvera Rico, remained. Rico, of course, was thoroughly interrogated.

He was quoted as follows: "Tomorrow, a *submarine* is to arrive for *me*."

Meanwhile, the press continued to have a field day. One leading Mexican newspaper dramatized the escape in a huge, one-word headline that read HELIFUGI-TIVES: "At this moment, the most spectacular search in all Mexican criminal history is in process. Units of the Army and Air Force are cooperating. Search parties are out over the entire length and breadth of the country. Highways are roadblocked and all vehicles passing through key points are being stopped. Interpol is alerted, all ports are being watched, the frontier towns guarded."

"Police theorize that the chopper landed on the roof of a house in Mexico City during the night and dropped off the two fugitives. There they were treated by a plastic surgeon and had new faces made for themselves to implement their escape," went another account.

"It must be assumed that the helicopter pilot was able to hypnotize the guards at Santa Marta," theorized a third.

In the midst of this furor, Melvin Belli came through with an interpretation of his client's legal position: "His escape was perfectly legal since jailbreaks are a crime in Mexico only if violence is used against prison personnel or property or if prison inmates or officials aid in the escape." As Vic would put it: "No one got a dime, that's what I love about it!"

Time magazine later summed it all up: "Kaplan seems to have pulled off a practically noncriminal crime."

37

Vic flew Joel west from Texas, heading for Judy's home in Santa Fe. Warily, however, Vic routed his flight plan to Sausalito. "Let the FBI look for you there," he told Joel.

At Santa Fe, Vic Stadter, the great rescue artist, master smuggler, and indomitable expediter, the genius of technical detail and split-second organization, proceeded to get lost, in broad daylight, en route from the airport via a rented car to Judy's home.

"Some goddamn bureaucrat must have shifted the road signs on me," he said.

Joel looked at his sister and neither of them could speak. "She stood in the doorway staring back at me, her eyes were all cloudy, then she sort of nodded and we embraced. I think that was the first time we ever did. We held each other for a long while. I could feel her tears along the side of my face. I don't suppose I will ever feel so much gratitude to anyone for as long as I live. What made it all so moving to us both, I suppose, was how little we had been a family. It was quite amazing. This girl was my sister but I'd hardly known her, not in the way one might suspect when one considers what she had done for me these last few years. We had come from parents who had never been close, from a father and uncles who hated each other, had really tried to destroy each other, but here was Judy, the daughter of these animosities, and there was all that love pouring out of her.

"I couldn't describe the way I felt. I hadn't had time to adjust to any of it. I suppose I was both elated and frightened. I was free but still very much on the run since I really didn't know who might be after me. I could easily be extradited if the powers so decided. I could also be killed, for I had far more powerful enemies than friends, and God knows I'd been threatened enough. I did not want to labor these fears, especially at such a tender and emotional time as this reunion, but I was always aware of them. The irony, again: if I should be captured now, or even worse, killed, after all these years and fortunes spent to free me.

"I saw Judy's children; the two youngest I had never met. They were beautiful and they were extremely warm to me. I'd sometimes worried how the children would respond to a convicted murderer, now an escaped convict. An uncle is not always a benevolent figure to a child, a fact to which I can readily testify. But Judy had filled them with moving thoughts of me, and they were easy to reach. I told them how they were the first children I had seen as a free man and how lucky I was that it was them. I believe they understood that."

At the Stadter house in Glendora, California, Mary was having unwelcomed visitors. Two persistent members of the FBI arrived to ask a few pertinent questions about the whereabouts of (a) her husband, and (b) his passenger in flight. She replied with her usual gentle charm that she did not know where Vic was, he had left several days before on a fishing trip with some friends and, since he was far out to sea, she had not heard from him. Nor did she know who this passenger might be. The name Joel Kaplan rang no bell in her memory.

The operative known to his intimates as Pussy was suffering in bed, wracked by the same persistent headache that had removed him from the action to which he had made such a contribution. He had heard nothing from Vic for almost a week, and for all his pain, he was deeply concerned about what was happening with the Kaplan caper. After all, it had dominated a year of his life: he'd made over twenty trips to Mexico City, moving in and out of Acatitla like a member of their staff, carrying all manner of contraband that was too risky for Irma, whom they watched closely. "Mostly, Joel had asked me to bring him books. Books about the sea and sailing and boats. He loved books about boats. He would give me titles that some stores never heard of, but sooner or later I'd find them. You'd think he was planning to sail out of that prison. As for contraband, the big thing was *Playboy* magazine."

In the midst of Pussy's sickbed ruminations, the phone rang; with his sixth sense, he knew it would be Vic.

"Pussy, my lad. . . ."

"Ah, you made it!"

"How are you?"

"Vic, you made it?"

"Are you feeling better?"

"*Vic! Did you make it?*"

"Well, hell, yes, what do you think?"

"I feel fine, Vic."

He would tell everyone over and over: that news was the best medicine he'd had in a week.

Vic checked with Mary before leaving Santa Fe. She told him the FBI were on the case and had Judy's Sausalito house under surveillance, but Glendora was clear. Vic decided to bring Joel to Glendora. Waiting for nightfall, he headed for a small, almost secret, landing strip at Upland, California; no radio, no facilities, "where everybody minds his own business." He called Mary again to be sure everything remained quiet and only then proceeded to sneak "his passenger" and himself into his own home.

38

Like Stadter himself, the house he lives in belonged in an earlier period. It is a magnificent old mansion with a decaying Bourbon plantation look, a huge house draped in the softness of Spanish moss and framed by old California oaks and sycamores. There are tall white columns on the seldom-used front entrance, green shutters on the windows; grass grows between the old stones of the shaded patio. All of this lies hidden, the outside world almost completely cut off from sight—except, at times, for the large rotating sign of the Alpha Beta Supermarket that peeks through a break in the trees, not three hundred yards from the property. To get to Vic's driveway, one has to cross a miniscule bridge at the rear of the supermarket's parking lot. It is a house that is not easy to find, which is the way Vic likes it.

Glendora is a small town backed into the San Fernando mountains on the northeastern tip of Los Angeles, frequently a trap for the worst smog attacks in the L.A. basin, a town of a few long straight blocks that hold the business center—one-story commercial buildings, taco and pizza stands, automobile sales and used-car lots with pennants flying, supermarkets, laundromats, cut-rate drug stores, all an impossible visual clash with the stately Stadter home.

258

It was at this mansion that the FBI set up what was to become an exceedingly irritating vigil. On the day after Joel's arrival, they returned to Glendora and again knocked on the door, and again Mary Stadter rejected them. "I wouldn't let them in the house, of course. They went to the boys working in the garage— Vic has a little side business manufacturing portable cement barbecue pits—and tried to find out if he and Joel were around." Failing there, the FBI men went to the county dump having somehow heard (correctly) that a mechanic employed there was another operative of Vic's and had once been dispatched to cash a $25,-000 check from Joel's sister. The man was Pussy and, unfortunately for the agents, he was not there. They then moved to the home of Vic's eighty-year-old mother; she was also uncooperative. When they asked permission to use her phone, she cut them off: "I told them I did not trust them with the instrument." Another contingent came nosing around the modest home of Roger Hershner, also of Glendora, but he, too, was not in—or so they were informed.

Joel, meanwhile, remained in the spacious Stadter home and rested, with Mary Stadter his hostess, cook, and nurse. "The man was in a terrible state," she recalls. "I'd never seen anyone so frightened. He was so pale, so weak. I wanted him to go to bed, but he simply could not rest there. Then his appendix scar became infected and was leaking pus."

Vic's Los Angeles doctor had died a few months before. He decided against calling one he did not trust, but took it on himself to handle the necessary treatment. "It was just a question of keeping the wound clean until the body healed itself. I put on a wet compress and bandaged him, and then made him sit still for a few days. We kept an eye on it."

Joel meanwhile, was keeping an eye on the agents outside who arrived daily to observe the house.

"I was annoyed by the way the FBI was after me.

I had violated no U.S. statutes. Extradition was not yet indicated. I was allegedly a free man but I could not live as one. They had absolutely no business being there at all, which, I suppose, may be the best explanation for their presence. They frightened me. I could see them through a crack in the curtains and I suspected they might actually make a move to kidnap me. More paranoia, perhaps, but the fear was as real as any. There was a laundry chute in the upper hall, a few feet from my bedroom. I made note of it the day I arrived and Vic showed me exactly where it dropped to, a large bin in the basement, right next to the washer and dryer. On one unforgettable afternoon, I was awakened from a nap by loud voices coming from the kitchen downstairs, and suspecting the worst, I made a quick move for that chute, worked my way into the small panel in the wall and slid down through the darkness of those inner walls. I am happy to report that the hubbub had nothing to do with me. I am even happier to report that there was a comfortable pile of dirty sheets waiting to soften my landing. Again, I was reminded that there are advantages to being small and underweight.

"It was a relief when the agents left a day or two later. When I could see that they were not about to return, I finally managed to risk a stroll around the grounds."

The house and grounds were guarded by two impressive-looking Great Danes whom Vic had trained to be hostile toward strangers. As Vic described them: "They were so tough-looking, I was sort of frightened of them myself. Then Joel got to them. By God, he treated them with such kindness, they got to licking his hand. They were no damn good to me after that."

For Joel, it was Irma's appearance in Glendora that he welcomed the most. She finally arrived with their eighteen-month old daughter, Aura Guadalupe Isabel Kaplan, that beautiful product of Mexico's more civilized approach to penal life.

Here was his wife of four years, loyal paramour of two more, a woman who had loved him through all the stormy years of what seemed like endless frustration and sickness. She was a real woman, he knew, having spent so much of his life with tinsel tramps and whores, nursing a sophomoric sense of what a woman was supposed to be. Now he could begin to make a decent life for her, to be husband and father, turning his energies toward something other than escape. In this triumphant mood, he took her into the moonlit bedroom like a newlywed, for this was the first time they had been together outside of a prison cell.

There was only one further disturbing moment after the FBI left: a collect phone call in the middle of the night for Joel Kaplan from Señor José Gonzales in San Luis Potosi.

The all-too familiar voice of Carlos Contreras Castro came bellowing across a thousand miles of wire:

"I'm in trouble, Joel!"

"What is it? Did they catch you?"

"Catch me? No. I need money!"

"Didn't Cotton give you $500?"

"My God, Joel—I spent that *last* week!"

39 The law offices of Melvin Belli are in the red brick Belli Building on Montgomery Street, a historic neighborhood that has been abruptly modernized by the construction of a Playboy Club on the corner just a few doors away. One of the few edifices of old town San Francisco to survive the earthquake and fire of 1906, the Belli Building remains a functioning symbol of the swashbuckling, romantic tradition of old San Francisco that local cynics say exists more in print than reality.

But even the cynics consider Belli something of an institution in the city. Belli's epic courtroom victories, which led him to be widely known as the "King of Torts," his flamboyant personal style, and his richly appointed Gold Rush era offices all contribute to the living legend.

Belli's personal office is as visible, and modest, as the Pyramids; it is at street level, an expanse of ornate French windows allowing passers-by a glance into the great man's room: it is a vista jammed with leather-covered law books, ancient typewriters, ferns, stuffed animals, a human skeleton, weapons, photographs—a potpourri of mementoes that would be difficult to duplicate in the average lifetimes of a dozen men. (When Belli seeks working moments away from the public eye, he retires to a basement inner room, less ornate but more functional.)

Belli's law partner in charge of the Kaplan affair, Vasilios Choulos, is a bright and resourceful attorney with a reputation for getting along equally well with oddballs and conservative bankers. At forty-five, Choulos is darkly handsome, sporting a flaring mustache and fashionable but not excessively mod clothes. Choulos, whose task it was to sort out the incredibly complex maneuvers behind the tangled estates of Joel and his sister Judy, is himself no stranger to familial wealth, being the son of a Greek immigrant grocer who made a million dollars in the food business. The attorney lives in suburban Mill Valley in a spectacular villa hidden from the road by tall shrubbery; statues of Greek goddesses dot the spacious grounds, and a pet boa constrictor resides in a glass cage in the kitchen.

The events of Choulos' own life have accustomed him to the bizzare and the unexpected, so he reacted calmly when an unlikely messenger appeared at the Belli Building just one week after Joel Kaplan's first helicopter flight.

At 11 o'clock on the morning of August 25, 1971, a "little old lady," gray-haired and somewhat stooped, speaking in a wheezing, cracked voice, presented herself to the Belli receptionist and asked to see Mr. Choulos. When asked her name, she replied that she only gave her name to people she trusted. In the meantime, she was here on business, and to prove it, opened her purse and withdrew a sealed envelope.

"Take this to Mr. Choulos, young lady," she said.

The receptionist passed the envelope to Choulos, who was on the phone, talking long distance to New York. Idly cradling the receiver under his jaw, he used both hands to open the envelope. When he saw what was inside, he immediately apologized to his party across the country and hung up.

He was looking at a polaroid snapshot of Joel David Kaplan dressed only in his jockey shorts and peering over the picture of Richard Nixon on the cover of the current issue of *Time* magazine.

"I'll see her immediately," he said to his secretary.

The little old lady sat down on a hard-backed chair, choosing to keep herself erect. He greeted her warmly, but she did not smile.

"All right, where is he?" Choulos asked.

She did not reply, but challenged him first.

"What is the phone number of Victor Stadter?"

He told her.

"And Mrs. Dowis?"

He told her that, too.

"All right, you're Choulos. He's here," she said, withdrawing a pen from her large purse and writing something on a piece of paper, which she passed across the desk.

The note had only three letters: "Vic."

Choulos smiled. "Why all the secrecy?"

"In case your place is bugged," she replied.

And when she rose to leave, he suddenly noted that the "little old lady" was not so old and, as she walked from his presence, his appreciative eye caught a glimpse of a figure that appeared to be more in the style of a diminutive Raquel Welch than Grandma Moses.

Vic apparently had all sorts of operatives. This one went by the name of Mary Milandra Stadter.

It was Vic's way of letting Choulos know his client was alive and well and anxious to chat.

Joel had a couple of things to chat about. First, there was the compelling question of his legal status and how he stood with regard to extradition by the Mexicans. Second, there was the matter of the money due him from his father's bequest.

264

Following instructions, Choulos flew to a southern California airport where, after flashing the proper recognition signal, he was accosted by Vic and spirited to the Glendora homestead. Joel and Choulos huddled. It was a long night.

The extradition possibility, Choulos would subsequently learn, was real, but the authorities were not pursuing it at any fevered pitch. The complete Joel Kaplan file was in the hands of the Mexican Foreign Ministry, and this agency was apparently aware that any move toward extradition would encounter vocal opposition, some of it from members of the U.S. Senate. As things stood, there was nothing Belli and Choulos could or should do about the problem.

The money was something they could do a great deal about. With their client "freely established" in the United States, Belli and Choulos took on the legal forces of Jack Kaplan. The pair of wildly plumed birds from San Francisco made a number of trips to New York, and, after six months of strained negotiations with their double-breasted Wall Street counterparts, suceeded in prying loose a portion of the moneys Joel claimed were owed him. More money is still at stake, and negotiations are expected to continue.

And the nightmare is not over. It pursues him wherever he goes. To the bright, neat garden apartment presided over by Irma and enlivened by their child. To the bars he frequents, sipping his bourbon and water.

It shows in his persistent use of a pseudonym, in his restlessness, in his sudden unexplained disappearances.

The threat that the FBI will come again in response to a Mexican extradition request is only the half of it. For, whatever the forces that framed him for the murder of Vidal and then levered the whole system of Mexican justice against him, they are presumably still operative.

Joel still wonders about those forces. The CIA? Right-wing Cubans? His dalliances with the Castro people would have been provocation enough for them. Uncle Jack? Certainly, with all his government contacts, including the CIA, he could have arranged it. Or did Uncle Jack use his influence to save Joel from a more terminal fate? Was prison the lesser punishment meted out to Joel because of his aid to Cuba's G-2?

Joel has the same answer to all these questions: perhaps.

40

Despite a generally enthusiastic press, Vic Stadter was not a happy man.

For one thing, Vic was being bombarded by calls from prospective clients as a result of all the publicity, but that same publicity was making it far more difficult for him to operate.

For another, his triumph was tainted by a failure: the chopper had never made it across the border. The loss had been avoidable, and that bothered him. He could sympathize with Roger Hershner's situation, yet he knew what he or Cotton would have done in similar circumstances. Confronting those Indians, for example, there was no reason to panic. He would have met them head on, a big smile, an offer of a drink. If they put their guns on him, wanting to take him to the police, he would have told the leader, sure, come on and ride in with me, I'll give you a ride in the chopper. No Indian could resist an offer like that; at least, he'd never met one who could. Then Vic would have taken him for a ride that would have ended somewhere north of the border—whereupon the Indian would be in trouble, not Vic. As for Roger's fear of being followed overhead, he was just "seeing ghosts." When a man runs scared, everyone is the enemy. Vic had been there before, too. Roger should have ignored that plane. And having lost

267

the radio frequency to United States Customs at Brownsville, he should have called in for the emergency frequency. Fifteen minutes more and he'd have been sitting at Brownsville airport with the $65,000 helicopter, prime asset of the Milandra Mining Company.

Vic had read about the mess in the Mexican papers —how Pedro Cortina, the milkman who had given Roger the ride, was arrested for doing so, even though he had betrayed Roger to the very police who later locked him up. Said Vic: "That's the way police are all over the world: if you rat on somebody, you're a rat through and through; you're likely to rat on them too, so they lock you up, it doesn't matter that you were only trying to help them."

For Vic, this was a gloomy ending that ate away at his hunger for perfection. It was a sad chain of events. He could not forgive his son-in-law for impeding his daughter from her normal filial duty. He had taken on the blonde in desperation and because of her incompetence and unreliability, he had been forced to waste Cotton to take care of Castro instead of sending him back with Hershner.

Contreras Castro, meanwhile, had been smuggled back to Venezuela where he rapidly achieved the status of an untouchable. What he told the hordes who sat nightly at his feet was not available for this record, but his first press conference gives some indication. To the assembled reporters of the Caracas media, he proudly declared that it was he, Carlos Contreras Castro, who had conceived and planned this greatest of all escapes. In fact, so valuable were his services, the millionaire Joel Kaplan had paid him $100,000 to lead them both out of their all-too-lengthy incarceration.

Joel read this dispatch via the wire services and was throughly amused.

Vic, however, did not think it funny at all.

ABOUT THE AUTHORS

Eliot Asinof's most recent book was *Craig and Joan: Two Lives for Peace*. Among his others are *Seven Days to Sunday* and *Eight Men Out*. Mr. Asinof is well known for his screen and television writing. Former editor of *Ramparts*, **Warren Hinckle** was also a moving force behind the short-lived *Scanlan's*. Mr. Hinckle is currently completing a memoir of the 1960's. For ten years, **William Turner** was an FBI agent. Since leaving the Bureau in 1961, Mr. Turner has written several books, including *J. Edgar Hoover and the FBI, Invisible Witness*, and *The Police Establishment*.

PHOTO CREDITS